Portable Document Reference Manual

Adobe Systems Incorporated

Tim Bienz and Richard Cohn

Tim Bienz and Richard Cohn
Adobe Systems Incorporated

M000289522

Addison-Wesley Publishing Company

Addison-Wesley Publishing Company
Reading, Massachusetts Menlo Park, California New York
Don Mills, Ontario Wokingham, England Amsterdam Bonn Sydney
Singapore Tokyo Madrid San Juan Paris Seoul Milan Mexico City Taipei

Library of Congress Cataloging-in-Publication Data

Portable document format reference manual / Adobe Systems Incorporated.
        p.   cm.
    Includes bibliographical references (p. 207) and index.
    ISBN 0–201–62628–4
    1. File organization (Computer science) 2. PostScript (Computer program language)
3. Text processing (Computer science) I. Adobe Systems.
QA76.9.F5P67   1993   93–8046
005.74—dc20   CIP

1 2 3 4 5 6 7 8 9–MA–9796959493

First Printing, June 1993

Contents

Section II: Optimizing PDF Files

Chapter 8: General Techniques for Optimizing PDF Files 113

Chapter 9: Optimizing Text 121

Chapter 10: Optimizing Graphics 131

Chapter 11: Optimizing Images 137

Figures

Tables

Examples

Section I

Portable Document Format

CHAPTER 1

Introduction

This book describes the Portable Document Format (PDF), the native file format of the Adobe™ Acrobat™ family of products. The goal of these products is to enable users to easily and reliably exchange and view electronic documents independent of the environment in which they were created. PDF relies on the imaging model of the PostScript™ language to describe text and graphics in a device- and resolution-independent manner. To improve performance for interactive viewing, PDF defines a more structured format than that used by most PostScript language programs. PDF also includes objects, such as annotations and hypertext links, that are not part of the page itself but are useful for interactive viewing.

PDF files are built from a sequence of numbered objects similar to those used in the PostScript language. The text, graphics, and images that make up the contents of a page are represented using operators based on those in the PostScript language, and closely follow the Adobe Illustrator™ 3.0 page description operators.

A PDF file is not a PostScript language program and cannot be directly interpreted by a PostScript interpreter. However, the page descriptions in a PDF file can be converted into a PostScript language program.

1.1 About this book

This book provides a description of the PDF file format, as well as suggestions for producing efficient PDF files. It is intended primarily for application developers who wish to produce PDF files directly. This book also contains enough information to allow developers to write applications that read and modify PDF files. While PDF is independent of any particular application, occasionally PDF features are best explained by the actions a particular application takes when it encounters that feature in a file. Similarly, Appendix D discusses some implementation limits in the Acrobat viewer applications, even though these limits are not part of the file format itself.

This book consists of two sections. The first section describes the file format and the second lists techniques for producing efficient PDF files. In addition, appendices provide example files, detailed descriptions of several predefined font encodings, and a summary of PDF page marking operators.

Readers are assumed to have some knowledge of the PostScript language, as described in the *PostScript Language Reference Manual, Second Edition*. In addition, some understanding of fonts, as described in the *Adobe Type 1 Font Format,* is useful.

The first section of this book, Portable Document Format, includes Chapters 2 through 7 and describes the PDF file format.

Chapter 2 describes the motivation for creating the PDF file format and provides an overview of its architecture. PDF is compared to the PostScript language.

Chapter 3 discusses the coordinate systems and transformations used in PDF files. Because the coordinate systems used in PDF are very much like those used in the PostScript language, users with substantial background in the PostScript language may wish to read this chapter only as a review.

Chapter 4 describes the types of objects used to construct documents in PDF files. These types are similar to those used in the PostScript language. Readers familiar with the types of objects present in the PostScript language may wish to read this chapter quickly as a reminder.

Chapter 5 provides a description of the format of PDF files, how they are organized on disk, and the mechanism by which updates can be appended to a PDF file.

Chapter 6 describes the way that a document is represented in a PDF file, using the object types presented in Chapter 4.

Chapter 7 discusses the page marking operators used in PDF files. These are the operators that actually make marks on a page. Many are similar to one or more PostScript language operators. Readers with PostScript language experience will quickly see the similarities.

The second section of this book, Optimizing PDF Files, includes Chapters 8 through 12 and describes techniques for producing efficient PDF files. Many of the techniques presented can also be used in the PostScript language. The techniques are broken down into four areas: text, graphics, images, and general techniques.

Chapter 8 discusses general optimizations that may be used in a wide variety of situations in PDF files.

Chapter 9 discusses optimizations for text.

Chapter 10 discusses graphics optimizations.

Chapter 11 discusses optimizations that may be used on sampled images.

Finally, Chapter 12 contains techniques for using clipping paths to restrict the region in which drawing occurs and a technique using images to make efficient blends.

1.2 Conventions used in this book

Text styles are used to identify various operators, keywords, terms, and objects. Four formatting styles are used in this book:

- PostScript language operators, PDF operators, PDF keywords, the names of keys in dictionaries, and other predefined names are written in boldface. Examples are **moveto**, **Tf**, **stream**, **Type**, and **MacRomanEncoding**.

- Operands of PDF operators are written in an italic sans serif font. An example is *linewidth*.

- Object types are written with initial capital letters. An example is FontDescriptor.

- The first occurrence of terms and the boolean values *true* and *false* are written in italics. This style is also used for emphasis.

Tables containing dictionary keys are organized with the **Type** and **Subtype** keys first, followed by any other keys that are required in the dictionary, followed by any optional keys.

1.3 A note on syntax

Throughout this book, Backus–Naur form (BNF) notation is used to describe syntax:

```
<xyz> ::=        abc <def> ghi |
                 <k> j
```

A token enclosed in angle brackets names a class of document component, while plain text appears verbatim or with some obvious substitution. The grammar rules have two parts. The name of a class of component is on the left of the definition symbol (::=). In the example above, the class is *xyz*. On the right of the definition symbol is a set of one or more alternative forms that the class component might take in the document. A vertical bar (|) separates alternative forms.

The right side of the definition may be on one or more lines. With only a few exceptions, these lines do not correspond to lines in the file.

The notation {...} means that the items enclosed in braces are optional. If an asterisk follows the braces, the objects inside the braces may be repeated *zero* or more times. The notation <...>+ means that the items enclosed within the brackets must be repeated *one* or more times.

When an operator appears in a BNF specification, it is shorthand for the operator plus its operands. For example, when the operator **m** appears in a BNF specification, it means *x y* **m**, where *x* and *y* are numbers.

Note that PDF is case-sensitive. Upper and lowercase letters are distinct.

CHAPTER **2**

Overview

Before examining the detailed structure of a PDF file, it is important to understand what PDF is and how it relates to the PostScript language. This chapter discusses PDF and its relationship to the PostScript language.

Chapter 3 discusses the coordinate systems used to describe various components of a PDF file. Chapters 4 and 5 discuss the basic types of objects supported by PDF and the structure of a PDF file. Chapters 6 and 7 describe the structure of a PDF document and the operators used to draw text, graphics, and images.

2.1 What is the Portable Document Format?

PDF is a file format used to represent a document in a manner independent of the application software, hardware, and operating system used to create it. A *PDF file* contains a *PDF document* and other supporting data.

A PDF document contains one or more pages. Each page in the document may contain any combination of text, graphics, and images in a device- and resolution-independent format. This is the *page description*. A PDF document may also contain information possible only in an electronic representation, such as hypertext links.

In addition to a document, a PDF file contains the version of the PDF specification used in the file and information about the location of important structures in the file.

2.2 Using PDF

To understand PDF, it is important to understand how PDF documents will be produced and used. As PDF documents and applications that read PDF files become more prevalent, new ways of creating and using PDF files will be invented. This is one of the goals of this book—to make the file format accessible so that application developers can expand on the ideas behind PDF and the applications that initially support it.

Currently, PDF files may be produced either directly from applications or from files containing PostScript page descriptions.

Many applications can produce PDF files directly. The PDF Writer, available on both Apple® Macintosh® computers and computers running the Microsoft® Windows™ environment, acts as a printer driver. A printer driver normally converts operating system graphics and text commands (QuickDraw™ for the Macintosh and GDI for Windows) into commands understood by a printer. The driver embeds these commands in a stream of commands sent to a printer that results in a page being printed. Instead of sending these commands to a printer, the PDF Writer converts them to PDF operators and embeds them in a PDF file, as shown in Figure 2.1.

Figure 2.1 *Creating PDF files using PDF Writer*

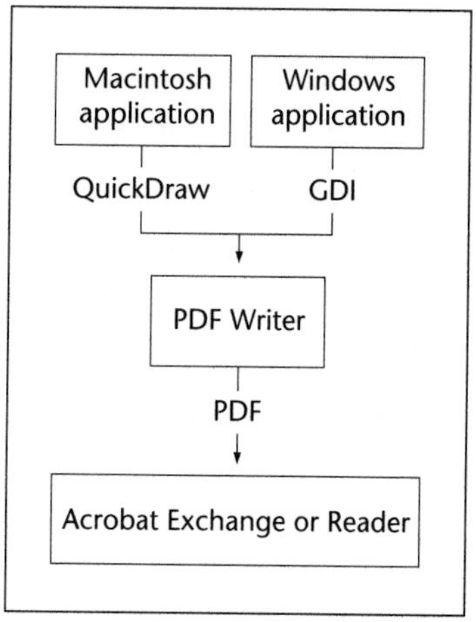

The resulting PDF files are platform-independent. Regardless of whether they were generated on a Macintosh or Windows computer, they may be viewed by a PDF viewing application on any platform.

Some applications produce PostScript page descriptions directly because of limitations in the QuickDraw or GDI imaging models or because they run on DOS or UNIX® computers, where there is no system-level printer driver. For these applications, PostScript page descriptions can be converted into PDF files using the Acrobat Distiller™ application, as shown in Figure 2.2. The Distiller application accepts any PostScript page description, whether created by a program or hand-coded by a human. The Distiller application produces more efficient PDF files than PDF Writer for some application programs.

Figure 2.2 *Creating PDF files using the Distiller program*

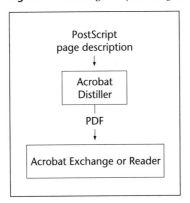

Once a PDF file has been created, Acrobat Exchange or Acrobat Reader can be used to view and print the document contained in the file, as shown in Figure 2.3. Users can navigate through the document using thumbnail sketches, hypertext links, and bookmarks. The document's text may be searched and extracted for use in other applications. In addition, an Acrobat Exchange user may modify a PDF document by creating text annotations, hypertext links, thumbnail sketches of each page, and bookmarks that directly access views of specific pages.

Figure 2.3 *Viewing and printing a PDF document*

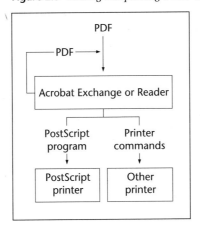

2.3 General properties

Given the goals and intended use of PDF, its design has several notable properties. This section describes those properties.

2.3.1 PostScript language imaging model

PDF represents text and graphics using the imaging model of the PostScript language. Like a PostScript language program, a PDF page description draws a page by placing "paint" on selected areas.

- The painted figures may be letter shapes, regions defined by combinations of lines and curves, or sampled images such as digitally sampled representations of photographs.

- The paint may be any color.

- Any figure can be clipped to another shape, so that only portions of the figure within the shape appear on the page.

- When a page description begins, the page is completely blank. Various operators in the page description place marks on the page. Each new mark completely obscures any marks it may overlay.

The PDF page marking operators are similar to the marking operators in the PostScript language. The main reason that the PDF marking operators differ from the PostScript language marking operators is that PDF is not a programming language and does not contain procedures, variables, and control constructs. PDF trades reduced flexibility for improved efficiency. A typical PostScript language program defines a set of high-level operators using the PostScript language marking operators. PDF defines its own set of high-level operators that is sufficient for describing most pages. Because these operators are implemented directly in machine code rather than PostScript language code, PDF page descriptions can be drawn more quickly. Because arbitrary programming constructs are not permitted, applications can more efficiently and reliably locate text strings in a PDF document.

2.3.2 Portability

A PDF file is a 7-bit ASCII file, which means PDF files use only the printable subset of the ASCII character set to describe documents—even those with images and special characters. As a result, PDF files are extremely portable across diverse hardware and operating system environments.

2.3.3 Compression

To reduce file size, PDF supports a number of industry-standard compression filters:

- JPEG compression of color and grayscale images

- CCITT Group 3, CCITT Group 4, LZW (Lempel-Ziv-Welch), and Run Length compression of monochrome images

- LZW compression of text and graphics.

Using JPEG compression, color and grayscale images can be compressed by a factor of 10:1 or more. Effective compression of monochrome images depends upon the compression filter used and the properties of the image, but reductions of 2:1 to 8:1 are common. LZW compression of text and graphics comprising the balance of the document results in compression ratios of approximately 2:1. All of these compression filters produce binary data, which is encoded in the ASCII base-85 encoding to maintain portability.

2.3.4 Font independence

Managing fonts is a fundamental challenge in document exchange. Generally, the receiver of a document must have the same fonts the sender used to create the document. Otherwise, a default font is substituted, producing unexpected and undesirable effects because the default font has different character metrics (widths) than the intended font. The sender could include the fonts with the document, but this can easily make even a short document quite large—a typical two-page memo using four fonts might grow from 10K to 250K. Another possibility is that the sender could convert each page of the document to a fixed-resolution image like a facsimile. Even when compressed, however, the image of a single page can be quite large (45–60K when sampled at 200-dpi). In addition, there is no intelligence left in the file, preventing the receiver from searching for or extracting text from the document.

PDF provides a new solution that makes a document independent of the fonts used to create it. A PDF file contains a *font descriptor* for each font used in a document. The font descriptor includes the font name, character metrics, and style information. This is the information needed to simulate missing fonts and is typically only 1–2K per font.

If a font used in a document is available on the computer where the document is viewed, it is used. If it is not available, a multiple master font is used to simulate on a character-by-character basis the weight and width of the original font, to maintain the overall "color" and formatting of the document. This solution applies to both Adobe Type 1 fonts and fonts in the TrueType™ format developed by Apple Computer, Inc.

Symbolic fonts must be handled in a special way. A symbolic font is any font that does not use the standard ISOLatin1 character set. Fonts such as Carta™, Adobe Caslon™ Swash Italic, Minion™ Ornaments, and Lucida® Math fall into this category. It is not possible to effectively simulate a symbolic font.

For symbolic fonts, a font descriptor (including metrics and style information) is not sufficient; the actual character shapes (or glyphs) are required to accurately display and print the document. For all symbolic fonts other than Symbol and ITC Zapf Dingbats®, a compressed version of the Type 1 font program for the font is included in the PDF file. Symbol and ITC Zapf Dingbats, the most widely used symbolic fonts, ship with Acrobat Exchange and Acrobat Reader and do not need to be included in a PDF file.

2.3.5   Single-pass file generation

Because of system limitations and efficiency considerations, it may be desirable or necessary for an implementation of a program that produces PDF such as the PDF Writer to create a PDF file in a single pass. This may be, for example, because the application has access to limited memory or is unable to open temporary files. For this reason, PDF supports single-pass generation of files. While PDF requires certain objects to contain a number specifying their length in bytes, a mechanism is provided allowing the length to be located in the file after the object. In addition, information such as the number of pages in the document can be written into the file after all pages have been written into the file.

2.3.6   Random access

Tools that extract and display a selected page from a PostScript language program must scan the program from its beginning until the desired page is found. On average, the time needed to view a page depends not only on the complexity of the page but also on the total number of pages in the document. This is problematic for interactive document viewing, where it is important that the time needed to view a page be independent of the total number of pages in the document.

Every PDF file contains a cross-reference table that can be used to locate and directly access pages and other important objects in the file. The location of the cross-reference table is stored at the end of the file, allowing applications that produce PDF files in a single pass to store it easily and allowing applications that read PDF files to locate it easily. Using the cross-reference table, the time needed to view a page in a PDF file can be nearly independent of the total number of pages in the document.

2.3.7 Incremental update

Applications may allow users to modify PDF documents, which can contain hundreds of pages or more. Users should not have to wait for the entire file to be rewritten each time modifications to the document are saved. PDF allows modifications to be appended to a file, leaving the original data intact. The addendum appended when a file is incrementally updated contains only the objects that were modified or added, and includes an update to the cross-reference table. Support for incremental update allows an application to save modifications to a PDF document in an amount of time proportional to the size of the modification instead of the size of the file. In addition, because the original contents of the file are still present in the file, it is possible to undo *saved* changes by deleting one or more addenda.

2.3.8 Extensibility

PDF is designed to be extensible. Undoubtedly, developers will want to add features to PDF that have not yet been implemented or thought of. For example, inclusion of audio and video data is not supported in version 1.0 of the file format. In addition, only simple text annotations are allowed—graphics cannot be included.

The design of PDF is such that not only can new features be added, but applications that understand earlier versions of the format will not completely break when they encounter features that they do not implement.

2.4 PDF and the PostScript language

The preceding sections mentioned several ways in which PDF differs from the PostScript language. This section summarizes these differences and describes the process of converting a PDF file into a PostScript language program.

While PDF and the PostScript language share the same basic imaging model, there are some important differences between them:

- A PDF file may contain objects such as hypertext links that are useful only for interactive viewing.

- To simplify the processing of page descriptions, PDF provides no programming language constructs.

- PDF enforces a strictly defined file structure that allows an application to access parts of a document randomly.

- PDF files contain information such as font metrics, to ensure viewing fidelity.

- PDF requires files to be represented in ASCII, to enhance document portability.

Because of these differences, a PDF file cannot be downloaded directly to a PostScript printer for printing. An application that prints a PDF file to a PostScript printer must carry out the following steps:

1. Insert *procsets*, sets of PostScript language procedure definitions that implement the PDF page description operators.

2. Extract the content for each page. Pages are not necessarily stored in sequential order in the PDF file. Each page description is essentially the script portion of a traditional PostScript language program using very specific procedures, such as "m" for **moveto** and "l" for **lineto**.

3. Decode compressed text, graphics, and image data. This is not required for PostScript Level 2 printers, which can accept compressed data in a PostScript language file.

4. Insert any resources, such as fonts, into the PostScript language file. Substitute fonts are defined and inserted as needed, based on the font metrics in the PDF file.

5. Put the information in the correct order. The result is a traditional PostScript language program that fully represents the visual aspects of the document, but no longer contains PDF elements such as hypertext links, annotations, and bookmarks.

6. Send the PostScript language program to the printer.

2.5 Understanding PDF

PDF is best understood by thinking of it in four parts, as shown in Figure 2.4.

Figure 2.4 *PDF components*

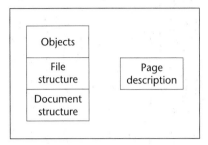

The first component is the set of basic object types used by PDF to represent objects. These types, with only a few exceptions, correspond to the data types used in the PostScript language. Chapter 4 discusses these object types.

The second component is the PDF file structure. The file structure determines how objects are stored in a PDF file, how they are accessed, and how they are updated. This structure is independent of the semantics of the objects. Chapter 5 explains the file structure.

The third component is the PDF document structure. The document structure specifies how the basic objects types are used to represent components of a PDF document: pages, annotations, hypertext links, fonts, and more. Chapter 6 explains the PDF document structure.

The fourth and final component is the PDF page description. A PDF page description, while part of a PDF page object, can be explained independently of the other components. A PDF page description has only limited interaction with other parts of a PDF document. This simplifies its conversion into a PostScript language program. Chapter 7 discusses PDF page descriptions.

CHAPTER 3

Coordinate Systems

Coordinate systems define the canvas on which all drawing in a PDF document occurs; that is, the position, orientation, and size of the text, graphics, and images that appear on a page are determined by coordinate systems.

PDF supports a number of coordinate systems, most of them identical to those used in the PostScript language. This chapter describes each of the coordinate systems used in PDF, how they are related, and how transformations among coordinate systems are specified. At the end of the chapter is a description of the mathematics involved in coordinate transformations. It is not necessary to read this section to use coordinate systems and transformations. It is presented for those readers who wish to gain a deeper understanding of the mechanics of coordinate transformations.

3.1 Device space

The contents of a page ultimately appear on a display or a printer. Each type of device on which a PDF page can be drawn has its own built-in coordinate system, and, in general, each type of device has a different coordinate system. Coordinates specified in a device's native coordinate system are said to be in *device space*. On pixel-based devices such as computer screens and laser printers, coordinates in device space generally specify a particular pixel.

If coordinates in PDF files were specified in device space, the files would be device-dependent and would accordingly appear differently on different devices. For example, images drawn in the typical device space of a 72 pixel per inch display and on a 600-dpi printer differ in size by more than a factor of 8; an eight-inch line segment on a display would appear as a one inch-segment on the printer. Different devices also have different orientations of their coordinate systems. On one device, the origin of the coordinate system may be at the upper left corner of the page, with the positive direction of the *y*-axis pointing downward. On another device, the origin may be in the lower left corner of the page with the positive direction of the *y*-axis pointing upward. Figure 3.1 shows an object that is two units high in device space, and illustrates the fact that coordinates specified in device space are device-dependent.

Figure 3.1 *Device space*

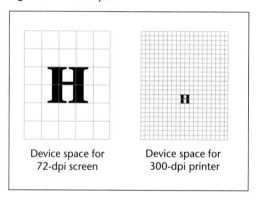

Device space for
72-dpi screen

Device space for
300-dpi printer

3.2 User space

PDF, like the PostScript language, defines a coordinate system that appears the same, regardless of the device on which output occurs. This allows PDF documents to be independent of the resolution of the output device. This resolution-independent coordinate system is called *user space* and provides the overall coordinate system for a page.

The transformation from user space to device space is specified by the *current transformation matrix* (CTM). Figure 3.2 shows an object that is two units high in user space and indicates that the CTM provides the resolution-independence of the user space coordinate system.

Figure 3.2 *User space*

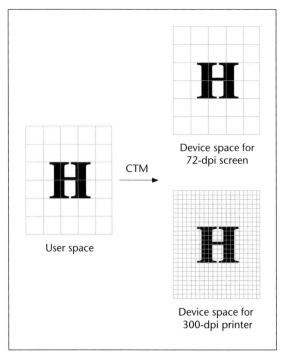

The user space coordinate system is initialized to a default state for each page of a document. By default, user space coordinates have 72 units per inch, corresponding roughly to the various definitions of the typographic unit of measurement known as the *point*. The positive direction of the *y*-axis points upward, and the positive direction of the *x*-axis to the right. The region of the default coordinate system that is viewed or printed can be different for each page, and is described in Section 6.4, "Page object."

3.3 Text space

The coordinates of text are specified in *text space*. The transformation from text space to user space is provided by a matrix called the *text matrix*. This matrix is often set so that text space and user space are the same.

3.4 Character space

Characters in a font are defined in *character space*. The transformation from character space to text space is defined by a matrix. For most types of fonts, this matrix is predefined except for an overall scale factor. (For details, see Section 6.8.2, "Font resources.") This scale factor changes when a user selects the font size for text.

3.5 Image space

All images are defined in *image space*. The transformation from image space to user space is predefined and cannot be changed. All images are one unit by one unit in user space, regardless of the number of samples in the image.

3.6 Form space

PDF provides an object known as a *Form*, discussed in Section 6.8.6, "XObject resources." Forms contain sequences of operations and are the same as forms in the PostScript language. The space in which a form is defined is *form space*. The transformation from form space to user space is specified by a matrix contained in the form.

3.7 Relationships among coordinate systems

PDF defines a number of interrelated coordinate systems, described in the previous sections. Figure 3.3 shows the relationships among the coordinate systems. Each line in the figure represents a transformation from one coordinate system to another. PDF allows modifications to many of these transformations.

Figure 3.3 *Relationships among PDF coordinate systems*

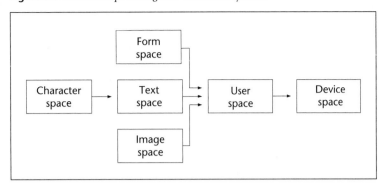

Because PDF coordinate systems are defined relative to each other, changes made to one transformation can affect the appearance of objects drawn in several coordinate systems. For example, changes made to the CTM affect the appearance of all objects, not just graphics drawn directly in user space.

3.8 Transformations between coordinate systems

Transformation matrices specify the relationship between two coordinate systems. By modifying a transformation matrix, objects can be scaled, rotated, translated, or transformed in other ways.

A transformations matrix in PDF, as in the PostScript language, is specified by an array containing six elements. This section lists the arrays used for the most common transformations. The following section contains more mathematical details of transformations, including information on specifying transformations that are combinations of those listed in this section.

- Translations are specified as [1 0 0 1 t_x t_y], where t_x and t_y are the distances to translate the origin of the coordinate system in x and y, respectively.

- Scaling is obtained by [s_x 0 0 s_y 0 0]. This scales the coordinates so that one unit in the x and y directions of the new coordinate system is the same size as s_x and s_y units in the previous coordinate system, respectively.

- Rotations are carried out by $\begin{bmatrix} \cos\theta & \sin\theta & -\sin\theta & \cos\theta & 0 & 0 \end{bmatrix}$, which has the effect of rotating the coordinate system axes by θ degrees counterclockwise.

- Skew is specified by $\begin{bmatrix} 1 & \tan\alpha & \tan\beta & 1 & 0 & 0 \end{bmatrix}$, which skews the x-axis by an angle α and the y-axis by an angle β. α and β are measured in degrees.

Figure 3.4 shows examples of each transformation. The directions of translation, rotation, and skew shown in the figure correspond to positive values of the array elements.

Figure 3.4 *Effects of coordinate transformations*

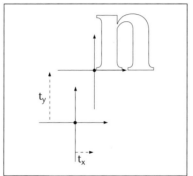

Translation

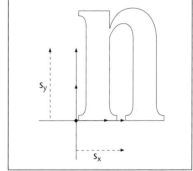

Scaling

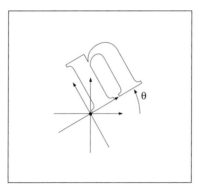

Rotation

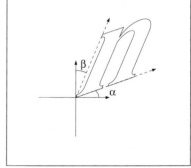

Skewing

If several transformations are applied, the order in which they are applied generally is important. For example, scaling the x-axis followed by a translation of the x-axis is not the same as first translating the x-axis, then performing the scaling. In general, to obtain the expected results, transformations should be done in the order: translate, rotate, scale.

Figure 3.5 shows that the order in which transformations are applied is important. The figure shows two sequences of transformations applied to a coordinate system. After each successive transformation, an outline of the letter "n" is drawn. The transformations in the figure are a translation of 10 units in the *x*-direction and 20 units in the *y*-direction, a rotation of 30 degrees, and a scaling by a factor of 3 in the *x*-direction. In the figure, the axes are drawn with a dash pattern having two units dash, two units gap. In addition, the untransformed coordinate system is drawn in light gray in each section. Notice that the scale–rotate–translate ordering results in a distortion of the coordinate system leaving the *x*- and *y*-axes no longer perpendicular, while the recommended translate–rotate–scale ordering does not.

Figure 3.5 *Effect of the order of transformations*

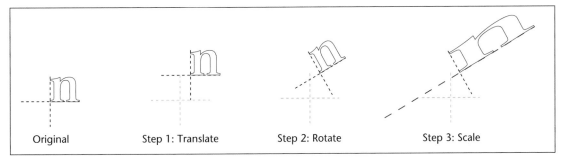

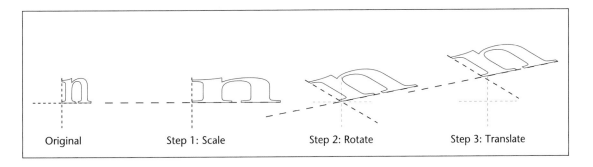

3.9 Transformation matrices

This section describes the mathematics of transformation matrices, which is identical to that underlying the PostScript language. It is not necessary to read this section to use the transformations discussed in previous sections.

To understand coordinate system transformations in PDF, it is vital to understand two points:

- Transformations in PDF alter coordinate systems, not objects. All objects drawn before a transformation is specified are unchanged by the transformation. Objects drawn after the transformation is specified will be drawn in the transformed coordinate system.

- Transformation matrices in PDF specify the transformation from the transformed (new) coordinate system to the untransformed (old) coordinate system. All coordinates used after the transformation are specified in the transformed coordinate system. PDF applies the transformation matrix to determine the coordinates in the untransformed coordinate system.

Note   *Many computer graphics textbooks consider transformations of objects instead of coordinate systems. Although both points of view are formally equivalent, some results differ depending on which point of view is taken.*

PDF represents coordinates in a two-dimensional space. The point *(x, y)* in such a space can be expressed in vector form as $\begin{bmatrix} x & y & 1 \end{bmatrix}$. Although the third element of this vector (1) is not strictly necessary, it provides a convenient way to specify translations of the coordinate system's origin.

The transformation between two coordinate systems is represented by a 3×3 transformation matrix written as:

$$\begin{bmatrix} a & b & 0 \\ c & d & 0 \\ e & f & 1 \end{bmatrix}$$

Note   *Because a transformation matrix has only six entries that may be changed, for convenience it is often written as the six-element array [a b c d e f].*

Coordinate transformations are expressed as:

$$\begin{bmatrix} x' & y' & 1 \end{bmatrix} = \begin{bmatrix} x & y & 1 \end{bmatrix} \begin{bmatrix} a & b & 0 \\ c & d & 0 \\ e & f & 1 \end{bmatrix}$$

Because PDF transformation matrices specify the conversion from the transformed coordinate system to the original (untransformed) coordinate system, x' and y' in this equation are the coordinates in the untransformed coordinate system, while x and y are the coordinates in the transformed system. Carrying out the multiplication:

$$x' = ax + cy + e$$

$$y' = bx + dy + f$$

If a series of transformations is carried out, the transformation matrices representing each of the transformations can be multiplied together to produce a single equivalent transformation matrix.

Matrix multiplication is not commutative—the order in which matrices are multiplied is significant. It is not *a priori* obvious in which order the transformation matrices should be multiplied. Matrices representing later transformations could either be multiplied before those representing earlier transformations (premultiplied) or after (postmultiplied).

To determine whether premultiplication or postmultiplication is appropriate, consider a sequence of two transformations. Specifically, apply a scaling transformation to the user space coordinate system and consider the conversion from this scaled coordinate system to device space. The two transformation matrices in this example are the matrix specifying the scaling (M_S) and the matrix specifying the transformation from user space to device space (the CTM, called M_C here). Recalling that coordinates are always specified in the transformed space, it is clear that the correct order of transformations must first convert the scaled coordinates to those in default user space, and then convert the default user space coordinates to device space coordinates. This can be expressed:

$$X_D = X_U M_C = (X_S M_S) M_C = X_S (M_S M_C)$$

where X_D is the coordinate in device space and X_U is the coordinate in default user space. This shows that when a new transformation is added, the matrix representing it must be premultiplied onto the existing transformation matrix.

This result is true in general for PDF—when a sequence of transformations is carried out, the matrix representing the combined transformation (M') is calculated by premultiplying the matrix representing the transformation being added (M_T) onto the matrix representing any existing transformations (M):

$$M' = M_T M$$

CHAPTER 4

Objects

The object types supported by PDF are similar to the object types supported by the PostScript language. Readers familiar with the PostScript language may wish to skim this chapter, or skip parts of it, particularly Sections 4.2, "Booleans," through 4.7, "Dictionaries."

4.1 Introduction

PDF supports seven basic types of objects: booleans, numbers, strings, names, arrays, dictionaries, and streams. In addition, PDF provides a null object. Objects may be labeled so that they can be referred to by other objects. A labeled object is called an *indirect object*.

The following sections describe each object type and the null object. A discussion of creating and referring to indirect objects in PDF files follows.

Note   *PDF is case-sensitive. Upper and lowercase letters are different.*

4.2 Booleans

The keywords **true** and **false** represent boolean objects with values *true* and *false*.

4.3 Numbers

PDF provides two types of numbers, integer and real. Integers may be specified by signed or unsigned constants. Reals may only be in decimal format. Throughout this book, *number* means an object whose type is either integer or real.

Note   *Exponential format for numbers (such as 1.0E3) is not supported.*

4.4 Strings

A string is a sequence of characters delimited by parentheses. If a string is too long to be conveniently placed on a single line, it may be split across multiple lines by using the backslash (\) character at the end of a line to indicate that the string continues on the following line. When this occurs, the backslash and end-of-line characters are not considered part of the string. Examples of strings are:

```
( This is string number 1? )

( strangeonium spectroscopy )

(This string is split \
  across \
three lines)
```

Within a string, the backslash character is used as an escape to specify unbalanced parentheses, non-printing ASCII characters, and the backslash character itself. This escape mechanism is the same as for PostScript language strings, described in Section 3.2.2 of the *PostScript Language Reference Manual, Second Edition*. Table 4.1 lists the escape sequences for PDF.

Table 4.1 *Escape sequences in strings*

\n	linefeed
\r	carriage return
\t	horizontal tab
\b	backspace
\f	formfeed
\\	backslash
\(	left parenthesis
\)	right parenthesis
\ddd	character code ddd (octal)

Use of the \ddd escape sequence is the preferred way to represent characters outside the printable ASCII character set, in order to minimize potential problems transmitting or storing the characters. The number ddd may contain one, two, or three octal digits. An example of a string with an octal character in it is:

```
(string with \245two octal characters\309)
```

As in the PostScript language, strings may also be represented in hexadecimal form. A hexadecimal string consists of a sequence of hexadecimal characters (the digits 0–9 and the letters A–F or a–f) enclosed within angle brackets (< and >). Each pair of hexadecimal digits defines one character of the string. If the final digit of a given string is missing—in other words, if there is an odd number of digits— the final digit is assumed to be zero. White-space characters (space, tab, carriage return, linefeed, and formfeed) are ignored. For example,

<901fa3>

is a three-character string consisting of the characters whose hexadecimal codes are 90, 1f, and a3. But:

<901fa>

is a three-character string containing the characters whose hexadecimal codes are 90, 1f, and a0.

4.5 Names

A name, like a string, is a sequence of characters. It must begin with a slash followed by a letter, followed by a sequence of characters. Names may contain any characters except linefeed, carriage return, %, (,), <, >, [,], {, and }. Examples of names are:

/Name1

/ASomewhatLongerName2

/A;Name_With-various***characters?.

4.6 Arrays

An array is a sequence of PDF objects. An array may contain a mixture of object types. An array is represented as a left square bracket ([ ), followed by a sequence of objects, followed by a right square bracket ( ]). An example of an array is:

[0 (Higgs) false 3.14 3 549 /SomeName]

4.7 Dictionaries

A dictionary is an associative table containing pairs of objects. The first element of each pair is called the *key* and the second element is called the *value*. Unlike dictionaries in the PostScript language, a key must be a name. A value can be any kind of object, including a dictionary. A dictionary is generally used to collect and tie together the attributes of a complex object, with each key–value pair specifying the name and value of an attribute.

A dictionary is represented by two left angle brackets (<<), followed by a sequence of key–value pairs, followed by two right angle brackets (>>). For example:

Example 4.1 *Dictionary*

```
<< /Type /Example /Key2 12 /Key3 (a string) >>
```

Or, in an example of a dictionary within a dictionary:

Example 4.2 *Dictionary within a dictionary*

```
<< /Type /AlsoAnExample
    /Subtype /Bad
    /Reason (unsure)
    /Version 0.01
    /MyInfo <<
        /Item1 0.4
        /Item2 true
        /LastItem (not!)
        /VeryLastItem (OK)
    >>
>>
```

Dictionary objects are the main building blocks of a PDF document. Many parts of a PDF document, such as pages and fonts, are represented using dictionaries. By convention, the **Type** key of such a dictionary specifies the type of object being described by the dictionary. Its value is always a name. In some cases, the **Subtype** key is used to describe a specialization of a particular type. Its value is always a name. For a font, **Type** is **Font** and four **Subtype**s exist: **Type1**, **MMType1**, **Type3**, and **TrueType**.

4.8 Streams

A stream, like a string, is a sequence of characters. However, an application can read a small portion of a stream at a time, while a string must be read in its entirety. For this reason, objects with potentially large amounts of data, such as images and page descriptions, are represented as streams.

A stream consists of a dictionary that describes a sequence of characters, followed by the keyword **stream**, followed by one or more lines of characters, followed by the keyword **endstream**.

```
<stream> ::=        <dictionary>
                    stream
                    {<lines of characters>}*
                    endstream
```

Table 4.2 shows the attributes of a stream.

Table 4.2 *Stream attributes*

Key	Type	Description
Length	integer	*(Required)* Number of characters from the first line after the line containing the **stream** keyword to the **endstream** keyword.
Filter	name or array of names	*(Optional)* Filters to be applied in processing the stream. The value of the **Filter** key can be either the name of a single decode filter or an array of filter names. Specify multiple filters in the order they should be applied to decode the data. For example, data compressed using LZW and then ASCII base-85 encoded can be decoded by providing the following key and value in the stream dictionary: /Filter [/ASCII85Decode /LZWDecode]
DecodeParms	variable	*(Optional)* Parameters used by the decoding filters specified with the **Filter** key. The number and types of the parameters supplied must match those needed by the specified filters. For example, if two filters are used, the decode parameters must be specified by an array of two objects, one corresponding to each filter. Use the null object for a filter's entry in the **DecodeParms** array if that filter does not need any parameters. If none of the filters specified requires any parameters, omit the **DecodeParms** key.

Streams may be filtered to compress them or convert binary streams into ASCII form. The standard PostScript Level 2 software decoding filters are supported. These filters and their parameters are listed in Table 4.3 and described in the following sections.

Table 4.3 *Standard filters*

Filter name	Parameters	Semantics
ASCIIHexDecode	none	Decodes binary data in an ASCII hexadecimal representation
ASCII85Decode	none	Decodes binary data in an ASCII base-85 representation
LZWDecode	dictionary	*(Parameters optional)* Decompresses text or binary data using LZW adaptive compression method
RunLengthDecode	none	Decompresses binary data using a byte-oriented run-length decoding algorithm
CCITTFaxDecode	dictionary	*(Parameters optional)* Decompresses binary data using a bit-oriented decoding algorithm, the CCITT facsimile standard
DCTDecode	dictionary	*(Parameters optional)* Decompresses sampled image data using a discrete cosine transform technique based on the JPEG standard

Example 4.3 shows a stream that has been compressed using LZW and then ASCII85 encoded, while Example 4.4 shows the same stream without any encoding.

Example 4.3 *Stream that has been LZW and ASCII85 encoded*

```
<<
/Length 528
/Filter [ /ASCII85Decode /LZWDecode  ]
>>
stream
J..)6T`?p&<!J9%_[umg"B7/Z7KNXbN'S+,*Q/&"OLT'FLIDK#!n`$"<Atdi`\Vn%
b%)&'cA*VnK\CJY(sF>c!Jnl@RM]WM;jjH6Gnc75idkL5]+cPZKEBPWdR>FF(kj1_
R%W_d&/jS!;iuad7h?[L-F$+]]0A3Ck*$l0KZ?;<)CJtqi65XbVc3\n5ua:Q/=0$W
<#N3U;H,MQKqfg1?:lUpR;6oN[C2E4ZNr8Udn.'p+?#X+1>0Kuk$bCDF/(3fL5]Oq
)^kJZ!C2H1'TO]Rl?Q:&'<5&iP!$Rq;BXRecDN[IJB`,)o8XJOSJ9sDS]hQ;Rj@!N
D)bD_q&C\g:inYC%)&u#:u,M6Bm%IY!Kb1+":aAa'S`ViJglLb8<W9k6YI\\0McJQ
kDeLWdPN?9A'jX*al>iG1p&i;eVoK&juJHs9%;Xomop"5KatWRT"JQ#qYuL,JD?M$
0QP)lKn06l1apKDC@\qJ4B!!(5m+j.7F790m(Vj8l8Q:_CZ(Gm1%X\N1&u!FKHMB~
>
endstream
```

Example 4.4 *Unencoded stream*

```
<<
/Length 558
>>
stream
2 J
BT
/F1 12 Tf
0 Tc 0 Tw 72.5 712 TD [ (Unencoded streams can be read easily)65 (,)] TJ
0 -14 TD [ (b)20 (ut generally tak)10 (e more space than \311)] TJ
```

```
T* (encoded streams.)Tj
0 -28 TD [ (Se)25 (v)15 (eral encoding methods are a)20 (v)25 (ailable in PDF)80 (.)]
TJ
0 -14 TD (Some are used for compression and others simply)Tj
T* [ (to represent binary data in an )55 (ASCII format.)] TJ
T* (Some of the compression encoding methods are suitable )Tj
T* (for both data and images, while others are suitable only )Tj
T* (for continuous-tone images.)Tj
ET
endstream
```

4.8.1 ASCIIHexDecode filter

This filter decodes data that has been encoded as ASCII hexadecimal.
ASCII hexadecimal encoding and ASCII base-85 encoding (described in
the following section) convert binary data such as images to the 7-bit
data required in PDF files. In general, ASCII base-85 encoding is
preferred because it is more compact.

ASCII hexadecimal encoding produces a 1:2 expansion in the size of
the data. Each pair of ASCII hexadecimal digits (0–9 and A–F or a–f)
produces one byte of binary data. All white-space characters are
ignored. The right angle bracket (>) indicates the end of data (EOD).
Any other character causes an error. If the filter encounters the EOD
marker after reading an odd number of hexadecimal digits, it behaves
as if a zero followed the last digit.

4.8.2 ASCII85Decode filter

This filter decodes data that has been encoded in the ASCII base-85
encoding and produces binary data.

ASCII base-85 encoding produces five ASCII printing characters from
every four bytes of binary data. Each group of four binary bytes
$(b_1\ b_2\ b_3\ b_4)$ is converted to a group of five encoded characters
$(c_1\ c_2\ c_3\ c_4\ c_5)$ using the relation:

$$(b_1 \times 256^3) + (b_2 \times 256^2) + (b_3 \times 256) + b_4 =$$

$$(c_1 \times 85^4) + (c_2 \times 85^3) + (c_3 \times 85^2) + (c_4 \times 85) + c_5$$

The five "digits" of the encoded base-85 number are converted to printable ASCII characters by adding 33 (the ASCII code for !) to each. The resulting data contains only printable ASCII characters with codes in the range 33 (!) to 117 (u).

Two special cases occur during encoding. First, if all five encoded digits are zero, they are represented by the character code 122 (z), instead of by a series of four exclamation points (!!!!). In addition, if the length of the binary data to be encoded is not a multiple of four bytes, the last partial 4-tuple is used to produce a last, partial output 5-tuple. Given n (1, 2, or 3) bytes of binary data, the encoding first appends $4 - n$ zero bytes to make a complete 4-tuple. This 4-tuple is encoded in the usual way, but without applying the special z case. Finally, only the first $n + 1$ characters of the resulting 5-tuple are written out. Those characters are immediately followed by the EOD marker, which is the two-character sequence ~>.

The following conditions are errors during decoding:

- The value represented by a 5-tuple is greater than $2^{32} - 1$.

- A z character occurs in the middle of a 5-tuple.

- A final partial 5-tuple contains only one character.

These conditions never occur in the output produced from a correctly encoded byte sequence.

4.8.3 LZWDecode filter

This filter decodes data encoded using the LZW data compression method, which is a variable-length, adaptive compression method. LZW encoding compresses binary and ASCII text data but always produces binary data, even if the original data was ASCII text. This binary data, in turn, must be converted to 7-bit data using either the ASCII hexadecimal or ASCII base-85 encodings described in previous sections.

LZW compression can discover and exploit many patterns in its input data, whether that input is text or image data. The compression obtained using the LZW method varies from file to file; the best case (a file of all zeroes) provides a compression approaching 1365:1 for long files, while the worst case (a file in which no pair of adjacent characters appears twice) can produce an expansion of approximately 2:3.

Data encoded using LZW consist of a sequence of codes that are 9 to 12 bits long. Each code represents a single character of input data (0–255), a clear-table marker (256), an EOD marker (257), or a table entry representing a multi-character sequence that has been encountered previously in the input (258 and greater).

Initially, the code length is 9 bits and the table contains only entries for the 258 fixed codes. As encoding proceeds, entries are appended to the table, associating new codes with longer and longer input character sequences. The encoding and decoding filters maintain identical copies of this table.

Whenever both encoder and decoder independently (but synchronously) realize that the current code length is no longer sufficient to represent the number of entries in the table, they increase the number of bits per code by one. The first output code that is 10 bits long is the one following creation of table entry 511, and so on for 11 (1023) and 12 (2047) bits. Codes are never longer than 12 bits, so entry 4095 is the last entry of the LZW table.

The encoder executes the following sequence of steps to generate each output code:

1. Accumulate a sequence of one or more input characters matching a sequence already present in the table. For maximum compression, the encoder looks for the longest such sequence.

2. Output the code corresponding to that sequence.

3. Create a new table entry for the first unused code. Its value is the sequence found in step 1 followed by the next input character.

To adapt to changing input sequences, the encoder may at any point issue a clear-table code, which causes both the encoder and decoder to restart with initial tables and a 9-bit code. By convention, the encoder begins by issuing a clear-table code. It must issue a clear-table code when the table becomes full; it may do so sooner.

The LZW filter can be used to compress text or images. When compressing images, several techniques reduce the size of the resulting compressed data. For example, image data frequently change very little from sample to sample. By subtracting the values of adjacent samples (a process called *differencing*) and LZW encoding the difference, rather than the raw sample values, a smaller output data size may be realized. Further, when the image data contains several color components (red–green–blue or cyan–magenta–yellow–black) per sample, taking the difference between the values of like components in adjacent samples, rather than between different color components in the same sample, often reduces the output data size. In order to control these and other options, the LZW filter accepts several optional parameters, shown in Table 4.4. All values supplied to the decode filter by any optional parameters must match those used when the data was encoded.

Table 4.4 *Optional parameters for LZW filter*

Key	Type	Semantics
Predictor	integer	If **Predictor** is 1, the file is decoded assuming that it was encoded using the normal LZW algorithm. If **Predictor** is 2, decoding is performed assuming that prior to encoding, the data was differenced. The default value is 1.
Columns	integer	Only has an effect if Predictor is 2. **Columns** is the number of samples in a sampled row. The first sample in each row is not differenced; all subsequent samples in a row are differenced with the prior sample. Each row begins on a byte boundary. Any extra bits needed to complete a byte at the end of a row (**Columns** × **Colors** × **BitsPerComponent**) are not differenced. The default value is 1.
Colors	integer	Only has an effect if **Predictor** is 2. Number of interleaved color components per sample in a sampled image. Each color component is differenced with the value of the same color component in the previous sample. Allowed values are 1, 2, 3, and 4. The default value is 1.
BitsPerComponent	integer	Only has an effect if **Predictor** is 2. **BitsPerComponent** is the number of bits used to represent each color component in a pixel. Allowed values are 1, 2, 4, and 8. The default value is 8.
EarlyChange	integer	If **EarlyChange** is 0, code word length increases are postponed as long as possible. If it is 1, they occur one code word early. The value of **EarlyChange** used in decoding must match that used during encoding. This parameter is included because LZW sample code distributed by some vendors increases the code word length one word earlier than necessary. The default value is 1.

The LZW compression method is the subject of United States patent number 4,558,302 and corresponding foreign patents owned by the Unisys Corporation. Adobe Systems has licensed this patent for use in its products. Independent software vendors (ISVs) may be required to license this patent to develop software using the LZW method to compress data for use with Adobe products. Unisys has agreed that ISVs may obtain such a license for a modest one-time fee. Further information can be obtained from Welch Licensing Department, Law Department, M/S C2SW1, Unisys Corporation, Blue Bell, Pennsylvania, 19424.

4.8.4   RunLengthDecode filter

This filter decodes data that has been encoded in a simple byte-oriented, run-length-encoded format. Run-length encoding produces binary data (even if the original data was ASCII text) that must be converted to 7-bit data using either the ASCII hexadecimal or ASCII base-85 encodings described in previous sections.

The compression achieved by run-length encoding depends on the input data. In the best case, a file of all zeroes, a compression of approximately 64:1 is achieved for long files. The worst case, the hexadecimal sequence of alternating 00 FF 00 FF, results in an expansion of 127:128.

The encoded data is a sequence of runs, where each run consists of a *length* byte followed by 1 to 128 bytes of data. If *length* is in the range 0 to 127, the following *length* + 1 (1 to 128 bytes) are copied literally during decompression. If *length* is in the range 129 to 255, the following single byte is to be copied 257 − *length* times (2 to 128 times) during decompression. The value 128 is placed at the end of the compressed data, as an EOD marker.

4.8.5   CCITTFaxDecode filter

This filter decodes image data that has been encoded using either Group 3 or Group 4 CCITT facsimile (fax) encoding. This filter is only useful for bitmap image data, not for color images, grayscale images, or text. Group 3 and Group 4 CCITT encoding produces binary data that must be converted to 7-bit data using either the ASCII hexadecimal or ASCII base-85 encodings, described in previous sections.

The compression achieved using CCITT compression depends on the data, as well as on the value of various optional parameters. For Group 3 one-dimensional encoding, the best case is a file of all zeroes. In this case, each scan line compresses to 4 bytes, and the compression factor depends on the length of a scan line. If the scan line is 300 bytes long, a compression factor of approximately 75:1 is achieved. The worst case, an image of alternating ones and zeroes, produces an expansion of 2:9.

CCITT encoding is defined by an international standards organization, the International Coordinating Committee for Telephony and Telegraphy (CCITT). The encoding is designed to achieve efficient compression of monochrome (1 bit per sample) image data at relatively low resolutions. The algorithm is not described in detail here, but can be found in the CCITT standards listed in the Bibliography at the end of this book.

The fax encoding method is bit-oriented, rather than byte-oriented. This means that, in principle, encoded or decoded data may not end on a byte boundary. The filter addresses this in the following ways:

- Encoded data are ordinarily treated as a continuous, unbroken bit stream. However, the EncodedByteAlign parameter (described in Table 4.5) can be used to cause each encoded scan line to be filled to a byte boundary. Although this is not prescribed by the CCITT standard and fax machines don't do this, some software packages find it convenient to encode data this way.

- When a filter reaches EOD, it always skips to the next byte boundary following the encoded data.

Both Group 3 and Group 4 encoding, as well as optional features of the CCITT standard, are supported. The optional parameters that can be used to control the decoding are listed in Table 4.5. Except as noted, all values supplied to the decode filter by the optional parameters must match those used when the data was encoded.

Table 4.5 *Optional parameters for CCITTFaxDecode filter*

Key	Type	Semantics
K	integer	Selects the encoding scheme used. A negative value indicates pure two-dimensional (Group 4) encoding. Zero indicates pure one-dimensional (Group 3, 1-D) encoding. A positive value indicates mixed one- and two-dimensional encoding (Group 3, 2-D) in which a line encoded one-dimensionally can be followed by at most **K** – 1 lines encoded two-dimensionally. The decoding filter distinguishes between negative, zero, and positive values of **K**, but does not distinguish between different positive **K** values. The default value is 0.
EndOfLine	boolean	End-of-line bit patterns are always accepted but required if **EndOfLine** is *true*. The default value is *false*.
EncodedByteAlign	boolean	If *true*, each encoded line must begin on a byte boundary. The default value is *false*.
Columns	integer	Specifies the width of the image in samples. If **Columns** is not a multiple of 8, the width of the unencoded image is adjusted to the next multiple of 8, so that each line starts on a byte boundary. The default value is 1728.
Rows	integer	Specifies the height of the image in scan lines. If this parameter is zero or is absent, the height of the image is not predetermined and the encoded data must be terminated by an end-of-block bit pattern or by the end of the filter's data source. The default value is 0.

EndOfBlock	boolean	If *true*, the data is expected to be terminated by an end-of-block, overriding the **Rows** parameter. If *false*, decoding stops when **Rows** lines have been decoded or when the data has been exhausted, whichever occurs first. The end-of-block pattern is the CCITT end-of-facsimile-block (EOFB) or return-to-control (RTC) appropriate for the **K** parameter. The default value is *true*.
BlackIs1	boolean	If *true*, causes bits with value 1 to be interpreted as black pixels and bits with value zero to be interpreted as white pixels. The default value is *false*.
DamagedRowsBeforeError		
	integer	If **DamagedRowsBeforeError** is positive, **EndOfLine** is *true*, and **K** is non-negative, then up to **DamagedRowsBeforeError** rows of data will be tolerated before an error is generated. Tolerating a damaged row means locating its end in the encoded data by searching for an **EndOfLine** pattern, and then substituting decoded data from the previous row if the previous row was not damaged or a white scan line if the previous row was damaged. The default value is 0.

4.8.6 DCTDecode filter

This filter decodes grayscale or color image data that has been encoded in the JPEG baseline format. JPEG encoding produces binary data that must be converted to 7-bit data using either the ASCII hexadecimal or ASCII base-85 encodings described in previous sections.

JPEG is a lossy compression method, meaning that some of the information present in the original image is lost when the image is encoded. Because of the information loss, only images (never text) should be encoded in this format. The compression achieved using the JPEG algorithm depends on the image being compressed and the amount of loss that is acceptable. In general, a compression of 15:1 can be achieved without a perceptible loss of information, and 30:1 compression causes little impairment of the image.

During encoding, several optional parameters control the algorithm and the information loss. The values of these parameters are stored in the encoded data, and the decoding filter generally obtains the parameter values it requires directly from the encoded data. A description of the parameters accepted by the encoding filter can be found in Section 3.13.3 of the *PostScript Language Reference Manual, Second Edition*.

JPEG stands for the ISO/CCITT Joint Photographic Experts Group, an organization responsible for developing an international standard for compression of color image data. The encoding method uses the discrete cosine transform (DCT). Data to be encoded consists of a stream of image samples, each containing one, two, three, or four color components. The color component values for a particular sample must appear consecutively. Each component value occupies an 8-bit byte.

The details of the encoding algorithm are not presented here but can be found in the references listed in the Bibliography. Briefly, the JPEG algorithm breaks an image up into blocks of 8×8 samples. Each color component in an image is treated separately. A two-dimensional DCT is performed on each block. This operation produces 64 coefficients, which are then quantized. Each coefficient may be quantized with a different step size. It is the quantization that results in the loss of information in the JPEG algorithm. The quantized coefficients are then compressed.

The amount of loss incurred in JPEG encoding is controlled by the encoding filter, which can reduce the loss by making the step size in the quantization smaller at the expense of reducing the amount of compression achieved by the algorithm. The JPEG filter implementation in the Acrobat products does not support features of the JPEG standard that are not relevant. In addition, certain choices regarding reserved marker codes and other optional features of the standard have been made.

4.9 The null object

The keyword **null** represents the null object.

Note *The value of a dictionary key can be specified as **null**. A simpler but equivalent way to express this is to omit the key from the dictionary.*

4.10 Indirect objects

A *direct object* is a boolean, number, string, name, array, dictionary, stream, or null, as described in the previous sections. An *indirect object* is an object that has been labeled so that it can be referenced by other objects. Any type of object may be an indirect object. Indirect objects are very useful; for example, if the length of a stream is not known before it is written, the value of the stream's **Length** key may be specified as an indirect object that is stored in the file after the stream.

An indirect object consists of an object identifier, a direct object, and the **endobj** keyword. The *object identifier* consists of an integer *object number*, an integer *generation number*, and the **obj** keyword:

```
<indirect object> ::=
                <object ID>
                <direct object>  ˙
                endobj
<object ID> ::=  <object number>
                <generation number>
                obj
```

The combination of object number and generation number serves as a unique identifier for an indirect object. Throughout its existence, an indirect object retains the object number and generation number it was initially assigned, even if the object is modified.

Each indirect object has a unique object number, and indirect objects are often but not necessarily numbered sequentially in the file, beginning with one. Until an object in the file is deleted, all generation numbers are zero.

4.11 Object references

Any object used as an element of an array or as a value in a dictionary may be specified by either a direct object or an indirect reference. An *indirect reference* is a reference to an indirect object, and consists of the indirect object's object number, generation number, and the **R** keyword:

```
<indirect reference> ::=
                <object number>
                <generation number>
                R
```

Using an indirect reference to the stream's length, a stream could be written as:

Example 4.5 *Indirect reference*

```
7 0 obj
<<
/Length 8 0 R
>>
stream
BT
/F1 12 Tf
72 712 Td (A stream with an indirect Length) Tj
ET
endstream
endobj
8 0 obj
64
endobj
```

CHAPTER 5

File Structure

This chapter describes the overall organization of a PDF file. A PDF file provides a structure that represents a document. This structure provides a way to rapidly access any part of a document and a mechanism for updating it.

The body of a PDF file contains a sequence of PDF objects that are used to construct a document. Chapter 4 describes the types of objects supported by PDF. Chapter 6 explains the way a document is constructed using these object types.

5.1 Introduction

A canonical PDF file consists of four sections: a one-line header, a body, a cross-reference table, and a trailer. Figure 5.1 shows this structure:

```
<PDF file> ::=      <header>
                    <body>
                    <cross-reference table>
                    <trailer>
```

All information in a PDF file is represented in ASCII. Binary data must be encoded in ASCII; ASCII hexadecimal and ASCII base-85 are supported. No line in a PDF file may be longer than 255 characters. A line in a file is delimited by a carriage return (ASCII value 13), a linefeed (ASCII value 10), or a carriage return followed by a linefeed. Updates may be appended to a PDF file, as described in Section 5.6, "Incremental update."

Figure 5.1 *Structure of a PDF file that has not been updated*

| Header |
| Body |
| Cross-reference table |
| Trailer |

5.2   Header

The first line of a PDF file specifies the version number of the PDF specification to which the file adheres. The current version is 1.0, for which the first line of a PDF file is **%PDF-1.0**:

<header> ::=   <PDF version>

5.3   Body

The body of a PDF file consists of a sequence of indirect objects representing a document. The objects, which are of the basic types described in Chapter 4, represent components of the document such as fonts, pages, and sampled images.

Comments can appear anywhere in the body section of a PDF file. Comments have the same syntax as those in the PostScript language; they begin with a % character and may start at any point on a line. All text between the % character and the end of the line is treated as a comment. Occurrences of the % character within strings are not treated as comments.

5.4 Cross-reference table

The cross-reference table contains information that permits random access to indirect objects in the file, so that the entire file need not be read to locate any particular object. For each indirect object in the file, the table contains a one-line entry describing the location of the object in the file.

A PDF file contains one cross-reference table, consisting of one or more sections. If no updates have been appended to the file, the cross-reference table contains a single section. One section is added each time updates are appended to the file.

The cross-reference section is the only part of a PDF file with a fixed format. This permits random access to entries in the cross-reference table. The section begins with a line containing the keyword **xref**. Following this line are one or more cross-reference subsections:

```
<cross-reference section> ::=
                xref
                <cross-reference subsection>+
```

Each subsection contains entries for a contiguous range of object numbers. The organization of the cross-reference section into subsections is useful for incremental updates, because it allows a new cross-reference section to be added to the PDF file, containing entries only for objects that have been added or deleted. Each cross-reference subsection begins with a header line containing two numbers: the first object number in that subsection and the number of entries in the subsection. Following the header are the entries, one per line:

```
<cross-reference subsection> ::=
                <object number of first entry in subsection>
                <number of entries in subsection>
                <cross-reference entry>+
```

Each entry is exactly 20 characters long, including the end-of-line marker. There are two formats for cross-reference table entries: one for objects that are in use and another for objects that have been deleted and so are free:

```
<cross-reference entry> ::=
                <in-use entry> |
                <free entry>
```

For an object that is in use, the entry contains a byte offset specifying the number of bytes from the beginning of the file to the beginning of the object, the generation number of the object, and the **n** keyword:

<in-use entry> ::=   <byte offset> <generation number> n

The byte offset is a ten-digit number, padded with leading zeros if necessary. It is separated from the generation number by a single space. The generation number is a five-digit number, also padded with leading zeros if necessary. Following the generation number is a single space and the **n** keyword. Following the keyword is the end-of-line sequence. If the end-of-line is a single character (either a carriage return or linefeed), it is preceded by a single space. If the end-of-line sequence is two characters (a carriage return followed by a linefeed), it is not preceded by a space.

For an object that is free, the entry contains the object number of the next free object, a generation number, and the **f** keyword:

<free entry> ::=   <object number of next free object> <generation number> f

The entry has the same format as that for an object that is in use: a ten-digit object number, a space, a five-digit generation number, a space, the **f** keyword, and an end-of-line sequence.

The free objects in the cross-reference table form a linked list, with the entry for each free object containing the object number of the next free object. The first entry in the table (object number 0) is always free and has a generation number of 65535. It is the head of the linked list of free objects. The last free entry in the cross-reference table (the tail of the linked list) uses 0 as the object number of the next free object.

When an indirect object is deleted, its cross-reference entry is marked free, and the generation number in the entry is incremented by one to record the generation number to be used the next time an object with that object number is created. Each time the entry is reused, its generation number is incremented. The maximum generation number is 65535. Once that number is reached, that entry in the cross-reference table will not be reused.

Example 5.1 shows a cross-reference section containing a single subsection with six entries; four that are in use (object numbers 1, 2, 4, and 5) and two that are free (object numbers 0 and 3). Object number 3 has been deleted, and the next object created with an object number of 3 will be given the generation number of 7.

Example 5.1 *Cross-reference section with a single subsection*

```
xref
0 6
0000000003 65535 f
0000000017 00000 n
0000000081 00000 n
0000000000 00007 f
0000000331 00000 n
0000000409 00000 n
```

Example 5.2 shows a cross-reference section with four subsections containing a total of five entries. The first subsection contains one entry, for object number 0, which is free. The second subsection contains one entry, for object number 3, which is in use. The third subsection contains two entries, for objects number 23 and 24, both of which are in use. Object number 23 has been reused, as can be seen from the fact that it has a generation number of 2. The fourth subsection contains one entry, for object number 30, which is in use.

Example 5.2 *Cross-reference section with multiple subsections*

```
xref
0 1
0000000000 65535 f
3 1
0000025325 00000 n
23 2
0000025518 00002 n
0000025635 00000 n
30 1
0000025777 00000 n
```

Appendix A contains a more extensive example of the structure of a PDF file after several updates have been made to it.

5.5 Trailer

The trailer enables an application reading a PDF file to quickly find the cross-reference table and certain special objects. Applications should read a PDF file from its end. The last line of a PDF file contains the end-of-file marker, **%%EOF**. The two preceding lines contain the keyword **startxref** and the byte offset from the beginning of the file to the beginning of the word **xref** in the last cross-reference section in the file. The trailer dictionary precedes this line. The trailer dictionary, shown in Table 5.1, consists of the keyword **trailer** followed by a set of key–value pairs enclosed in double angle brackets:

```
<trailer> ::=        trailer
                     <<
                     <trailer key–value pair>+
                     >>
                     startxref
                     <cross-reference table start address>
                     %%EOF
```

Table 5.1 *Trailer attributes*

Key	Type	Semantics
Size	integer	*(Required)* Total number of entries in the file's cross-reference table, including the original table and all updates.
Prev	integer	*(Present only if the file has more than one cross-reference section)* Byte offset from the beginning of file to the location of the previous cross-reference section. If the file has never been updated, it will not contain the **Prev** key.
Root	dictionary	*(Required; must be indirect reference)* Catalog object for the document, described in Section 6.2, "Catalog."
Info	dictionary	*(Optional; must be indirect reference)* Info dictionary for the document, described in Section 6.9, "Info dictionary."

An example trailer for a file that has not been updated is shown in Example 5.3. The fact that the file has not been updated is determined from the absence of a **Prev** key in the trailer dictionary.

Example 5.3 *Trailer*

```
trailer
<<
/Size 22
/Root 2 0 R
/Info 1 0 R
>>
startxref
18799
%%EOF
```

5.6 Incremental update

The contents of a PDF file can be updated without rewriting the entire file. Changes can be appended to the end of the file, leaving completely intact the original contents of the file. When a PDF file is updated, any new or changed objects are appended, a cross-reference section is added, and a new trailer is inserted. The resulting file has the structure shown in Figure 5.2:

```
<Updated PDF file> ::=
                        <PDF file>
                        {<update>}*
<update> ::=            <body>
                        <cross-reference section>
                        <trailer>
```

A complete example of an updated file is shown in Appendix A.

The cross-reference section added when a PDF file is updated contains entries only for objects that have been changed, replaced, or deleted. Deleted objects are left unchanged in the file, but are marked as deleted in their cross-reference entries. The trailer that is added contains all the information in the previous trailer, as well as a **Prev** key specifying the location of the previous cross-reference section. As shown in Figure 5.2, after a file has been updated several times it contains several trailers, as well as several **%%EOF** lines.

Because updates are appended to PDF files, it is possible to end up with several copies of an object with the same object ID (object number and generation number) in a file. This occurs, for example, if a text annotation is changed several times, with the file being saved between changes. Because the text annotation object is not deleted, it retains the same object number and generation number. Because it has been changed, however, an updated copy of the object is included in the update section added to the file. The cross-reference section added includes a pointer to this new changed version, overriding the information contained in the original cross-reference section. When the file is read, cross-reference information is built in such a way that the most recent version of an object is accessed in the file.

Figure 5.2 *Structure of a PDF file after changes have been appended several times*

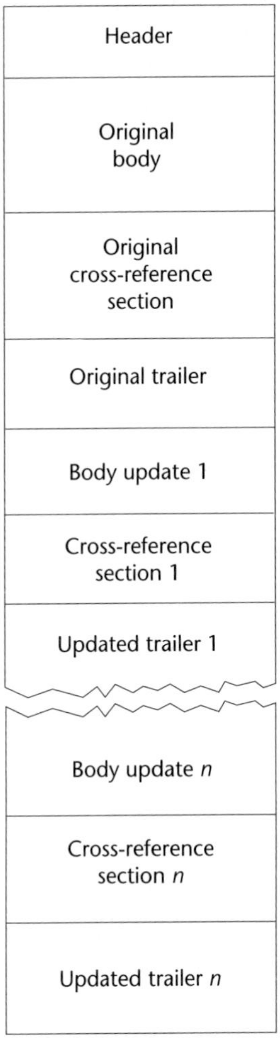

Header
Original body
Original cross-reference section
Original trailer
Body update 1
Cross-reference section 1
Updated trailer 1
~~
Body update *n*
Cross-reference section *n*
Updated trailer *n*

CHAPTER 6

Document Structure

PDF provides an electronic representation of a document—a series of pages containing text, graphics, and images, along with other information such as thumbnails (miniature images of the pages), text annotations, hypertext links, and outline entries (also called bookmarks). Previous chapters lay the groundwork for understanding the PDF representation of a document, but do not describe the representation itself. Chapter 3 presents the coordinate systems that provide the supports on which the visible part of a PDF document depends. Chapter 4 explains the types of objects supported by PDF. Document components used in PDF are built from those objects. Chapter 5 describes the overall structure of a PDF file, which provides the framework necessary to organize the pieces of a document, move rapidly among the pages of a document, and update a document.

The body of a PDF file consists of a sequence of objects that collectively represent a PDF document. This chapter focuses exclusively on the contents of the body section of a PDF file and contains a description of each type of object that may be contained in a PDF document. Following each description is an example showing the object as it might appear in a PDF file. Complete example PDF files appear in Appendix A.

6.1 Introduction

A PDF document can be described as a hierarchy of objects contained in the body section of a PDF file. Figure 6.1 shows the structure of a PDF document. Most objects in this hierarchy are dictionaries. Parent, child, and sibling relationships are represented by key–value pairs whose values are indirect references to parent, child, or sibling objects. For example, the Catalog object, which is the root of the hierarchy, contains a Pages key whose value is an indirect reference to the object that is the root of the Pages tree.

Each page of the document includes references to its imageable contents, its thumbnail, and any annotations that appear on the page. The PDF file's standard trailer, described in Section 5.5, "Trailer," specifies the location of the Catalog object as the value of the trailer's **Root** key. In addition, the trailer specifies the location of the document's Info dictionary, a structure that contains general information about the document, as the value of the trailer's **Info** key.

Note   *In many of the tables in this chapter, certain key–value pairs contain the notation "must be an indirect reference" or "indirect reference preferred." Unless one of these is specified in the description of the key–value pair, objects that are the value of a key can either be specified directly or using an indirect reference, as described in Section 4.11, "Object references."*

Figure 6.1 *Structure of a PDF document*

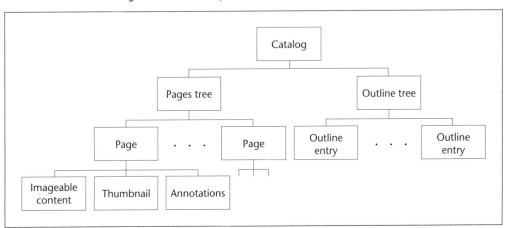

6.2   Catalog

The Catalog is a dictionary that is the root node of the document. It contains a reference to the tree of pages contained in the document, and a reference to the tree of objects representing the document's outline. In addition, the Catalog indicates whether the document's outline or thumbnail page images should be displayed automatically when the document is viewed. Example 6.1 shows a sample Catalog object.

Example 6.1 *Catalog*

```
1 0 obj
<<
/Type /Catalog
/Pages 2 0 R
/Outlines 3 0 R
/PageMode /UseOutlines
>>
endobj
```

Table 6.1 shows the attributes for a Catalog.

Table 6.1 *Catalog attributes*

Key	Type	Semantics
Type	name	*(Required)* Object type. Always **Catalog**.
Pages	dictionary	*(Required, must be an indirect reference)* Pages object that is the root of the document's Pages tree.
Outlines	dictionary	*(Required if the document has an outline, must be an indirect reference)* Outlines object that is the root of the document's outline tree, described in Section 6.7, "Outline tree."
PageMode	name	*(Optional)* Specifies how the document should appear when opened. Allowed values: **UseNone**—Open document with neither outline nor thumbnails visible **UseOutlines**—Open document with outline visible **UseThumbs**—Open document with thumbnails visible The default **PageMode** is **UseNone**.

6.3 Pages tree

The pages of a document are accessible through a tree of nodes known as the Pages tree. This tree defines the ordering of the pages in the document.

To optimize the performance of viewer applications, the Acrobat Distiller program and Acrobat PDF Writer construct balanced trees with each node in the tree containing up to six children. (For further information on balanced trees, see the Bibliography.) The tree structure allows applications to quickly open a document containing thousands of pages using only limited memory. Applications should accept any sort of tree structure as long as the nodes of the tree contain the keys described in Table 6.2. The simplest structure consists of a single Pages node that references all the page objects directly.

The root and all interior nodes of the Pages tree are dictionaries, whose minimum contents are shown in Table 6.2. A Pages object may contain additional keys that provide default values for keys of the same name in pages that are descendants of the Pages object. For example, a document may specify a **MediaBox** for all pages by defining one in the root Pages object. An individual page in the document could override the **MediaBox** in this example by including a **MediaBox** in the Page object for that page.

Table 6.2 *Pages attributes*

Key	Type	Semantics
Type	name	*(Required)* Object type. Always **Pages**.
Kids	array	*(Required)* List of indirect references to the immediate children of this Pages node.
Count	integer	*(Required)* Specifies the number of leaf nodes (imageable pages) under this node. The leaf nodes do not have to be immediately below this node in the tree, but can be several levels deeper in the tree.
Parent	dictionary	*(Required; must be indirect reference)* Pages object that is the immediate ancestor of this Pages object. The root Pages object has no **Parent**.

Example 6.2 illustrates the Pages object for a document with three pages, while Appendix A contains an example showing the Pages tree for a document containing 62 pages.

Example 6.2 *Pages tree for a document containing three pages*

```
2 0 obj
<<
/Type /Pages
/Kids [ 4 0 R 10 0 R 24 0 R ]
/Count 3
>>
endobj
```

6.4 Page objects

A Page object is a dictionary whose keys describe a single page containing text, graphics and images. A Page object is a leaf of the Pages tree, and has the attributes shown in Table 6.3.

Table 6.3 *Page attributes*

Key	Type	Semantics
Type	name	*(Required)* Object type. Always **Page**.
MediaBox	array	*(Required)* Rectangle specifying the "natural size" of the page, for example the dimensions of an A4 sheet of paper. The rectangle is an array of four integers that specify the x- and y-coordinates of the lower left corner and the x- and y-coordinates of the upper right corner of the page, in that order. The coordinates are measured in default user space units.
Parent	dictionary	*(Required; must be indirect reference)* Pages object that is the immediate ancestor of this page.
Resources	dictionary	*(Required unless Page has no resources)* Resources required by this page, described in Section 6.8, "Resources."
Contents	stream or array	*(Optional; must be indirect reference)* The page description (contents) for this page, described in Chapter 7. If **Contents** is an array of streams, they are concatenated to produce the page description. This allows a program that is creating a PDF file to create image objects and other resources as they occur, even though they interrupt the page description. If **Contents** is absent, the page is empty.
CropBox	array	*(Optional)* Rectangle specifying the region of the page displayed and printed. The rectangle is specified in the same way as **MediaBox**.
Rotate	integer	*(Optional)* Specifies the number of degrees the page should be rotated clockwise when it is displayed. This value must be zero (the default) or a multiple of 90.
Thumb	stream	*(Optional; must be indirect reference)* Object that contains a thumbnail sketch of the page, described in Section 6.5, "Thumbnails."
Annots	array	*(Optional)* An array of objects, each representing an annotation on the page, described in Section 6.6, "Annotations." Omit the **Annots** key if the page has no annotations.

Certain attributes can be omitted from a Page object, and their value inherited from a Pages object that is an ancestor of the Page. These attributes are **CropBox**, **MediaBox**, **Resources**, and **Rotate**.

Figure 6.2 shows the distinction between the media box and the crop box. In the figure, the crop box has been sized so that the crop marks do not appear when the page is viewed or printed.

Note   *The intersection between the page's media box and the crop box is the region of the default user space coordinate system that is viewed or printed. Typically, the crop box is located entirely inside the media box, so that the intersection is the same as the crop box itself.*

Figure 6.2 *Page object's media box and crop box*

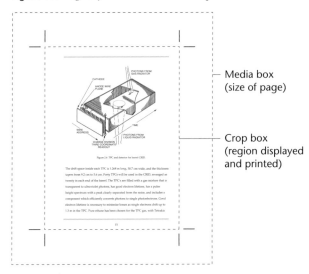

Example 6.3 shows a Page object with a thumbnail and two annotations. In addition, the Resources dictionary is specified as a direct object, and shows that the page makes use of three fonts, with the names F3, F5, and F7.

Example 6.3 *Page with thumbnail, annotations, and Resources dictionary*

```
3 0 obj
<<
/Type /Page
/Parent 4 0 R
/MediaBox [ 0 0 612 792 ]
/Resources << /Font << /F3 7 0 R /F5 9 0 R /F7 11 0 R >> >>
/Thumb 12 0 R
/Contents 14 0 R
/Annots [ 23 0 R 24 0 R ]
>>
endobj
```

6.5 Thumbnails

A PDF document may include thumbnail sketches of its pages. They are not required, and even if some pages have them, others may not.

The thumbnail image for a page is the value of the **Thumb** key of the page object. The structure of a thumbnail is very similar to that of an image resource (see Section 6.8.6, "XObject resources.") The only difference between a thumbnail and an image resource is that a thumbnail does not include **Type**, **Subtype**, and **Name** keys.

Note *Different pages in a document may have thumbnails with different numbers of bits per color component.*

Example 6.4 *Thumbnail*

```
12 0 obj
<<
/Filter [ /ASCII85Decode /DCTDecode  ]
/Width 76
/Height 99
/BitsPerComponent 8
/ColorSpace /DeviceRGB
/Length 13 0 R
>>
stream
s4IA>!"M;*Ddm8XA,IT0!!3,S!/(=R!<E3%!<N<(!WrK*!WrN,!
... much omitted image data...
C:20"A(p4YlM$B@Eme1Y7Z;J4$cc=Lj/]5#e^_1plJ-N)DE>A<*F2m0Y-
endstream
endobj
13 0 obj
4298
endobj
```

6.6 Annotations

Annotations are notes or other objects that are associated with a page but are separate from the page description itself. PDF currently supports two kinds of annotations: text notes and hypertext links. In the future it may support additional types such as sound and graphics.

If a page includes annotations, they are stored in an array as the value of the **Annots** key of the page object. Each annotation is a dictionary. All annotations must provide a core set of keys, including the **Type**, **Subtype**, and **Rect** keys.

Note   *All coordinates and measurements in text annotations, link annotations, and outline entries are specified in default user space units. Where a rectangle is specified as an array of integers, it is in the form:*

$$[x_{\text{lower left}} \ y_{\text{lower left}} \ x_{\text{upper right}} \ y_{\text{upper right}}]$$

6.6.1   Text annotations

A text annotation contains a string of text. When the annotation is open, the text is displayed. A PDF viewer application chooses the size and typeface of the text. Text can be separated into paragraphs using carriage returns. Table 6.4 shows the contents of the text annotation dictionary.

Table 6.4 *Text annotation attributes*

Key	Type	Semantics
Type	name	*(Required)* Object type. Always **Annot**.
Subtype	name	*(Required)* Annotation subtype. Always **Text**.
Rect	array of integers	*(Required)* Rectangle specifying the location of the annotation.
Contents	string	*(Required)* The text to be displayed. The characters in this string are encoded using the predefined encoding **PDFDocEncoding**, described in Appendix C.
Open	boolean	*(Optional)* If *true*, specifies that the annotation should be initially displayed opened. The default is *false* (closed).

Example 6.5 shows a text annotation.

Example 6.5 *Text annotation*

```
22 0 obj
<<
/Type /Annot
/Subtype /Text
/Rect [ 266 116 430 204 ]
/Contents (text for two)
>>
endobj
```

6.6.2   Link annotations

A link annotation, when activated, displays the view specified in the annotation. The view may be of a location on a different page and have a different zoom factor. Table 6.5 shows the contents of the link annotation dictionary.

Table 6.5 *Link annotation attributes*

Key	Type	Semantics
Type	name	*(Required)* Object type. Always **Annot**.
Subtype	name	*(Required)* Annotation subtype. Always **Link**.
Rect	array of integers	*(Required)* Rectangle specifying the location of the annotation.
Dest	array	*(Required)* The view to go to, as described in Table 6.6.
Border	array of numbers	*(Optional)* Three numbers specifying the horizontal corner radius, the vertical corner radius, and the width of the border of the annotation. The default values are 0, 0, and 1, respectively. No border is drawn if the width is 0.

Example 6.6 shows a link annotation.

Example 6.6 *Link annotation*

```
93 0 obj
<<
/Type /Annot
/Subtype /Link
/Rect [ 71 717 190 734 ]
/Border [ 16 16 1 ]
/Dest [ 3 0 R /FitR -4 399 199 533 ]
>>
endobj
```

6.6.3   Destinations

Link annotations and outline entries specify a destination, which consists of a page, the location of the display window on the destination page, and the zoom factor to use when displaying the destination page. The destination is represented as an array containing an indirect reference to the page object which is the destination page, along with other information needed to specify the location and zoom.

Table 6.6 shows the allowed forms of the destination. In the table *top*, *left*, *right*, and *bottom* are numbers specified in the default user space coordinate system. *page* is an indirect reference to the destination Page object.

Table 6.6 *Annotation destination specification*

Value of /Dest key	Semantics
[*page* /XYZ *left top zoom*]	*left* and *top* specify the coordinates of the top left corner of the window. If *left*, *top*, or *zoom* is null, the current value of that parameter is retained. For example, specifying a destination as [4 0 R null null null] will go to the page object with an object ID of 4 0, retaining the same *top*, *left*, and *zoom* as the current page. A zoom of 0 has the same meaning as a zoom of null.
[*page* /Fit]	Fit the page to the window.
[*page* /FitH *top*]	Fit the width of the page to the window. *top* specifies the *y*-coordinate of the top of the window.
[*page* /FitV *left*]	Fit the height of the page to the window. *left* specifies the *x*-coordinate of the left edge of the window.
[*page* /FitR *left bottom right top*]	Fit the rectangle specified by *left bottom right top* in the window. If *top* – *bottom* and *right* – *left* imply different zoom factors, the numerically smaller zoom is used, to ensure that the specified rectangle fits in the window.

6.7   Outline tree

An outline allows a user to access views of a document by name. As with a link annotation, activation of an outline entry (also called a *bookmark*) brings up a new view based on the destination description. Outline entries form a hierarchy of elements. An entry may be one of several at the same level in the outline, it may be a sub-entry of another entry, and it may have its own set of child entries. An outline entry may be open or closed. If it is open, its immediate children are visible when the outline is displayed. If it is closed, they are not.

If a document includes an outline, it is accessed from the **Outlines** key in the Catalog object. The value of this key is the Outlines object, which is the root of the outline tree. The contents of the Outlines dictionary appear in Table 6.7 and Example 6.7. The top-level outline entries are contained in a linked list with **First** pointing to the head of the list and **Last** pointing to the tail of the list. When displayed, outline entries appear in the order in which they occur in the linked list.

Table 6.7 *Outlines attributes*

Key	Type	Semantics
Count	integer	(*Required if document has any outline entries*) Total number of open entries in the outline. This includes the total number of items open at all outline levels, not just top-level outline entries. If the count is zero, this key should be omitted.
First	dictionary	(*Required if document has any outline entries; must be indirect reference*) Reference to the outline entry that is the head of the linked list of top-level outline entries.
Last	dictionary	(*Required if document has any outline entries; must be indirect reference*) Reference to the outline entry that is the tail of the linked list of top-level outline entries.

Example 6.7 *Outlines object with six open entries*

```
21 0 obj
<<
/Count 6
/First 22 0 R
/Last 29 0 R
>>
endobj
```

Each outline entry is a dictionary, whose contents are shown in Table 6.8.

Table 6.8 *Outline entry attributes*

Key	Type	Semantics
Title	string	(*Required*) The text that appears in the outline for this entry. The characters in this string are encoded using the predefined encoding **PDFDocEncoding**, described in Appendix C.
Dest	array	(*Required*) A view that uses the same format as views that are part of link annotations, as described in Table 6.6.
Parent	dictionary	(*Required; must be indirect reference*) Specifies the entry that the current entry is a sub-entry of. The parent of the top-level entries is the Outlines object.
Prev	dictionary	(*Required if the entry is not the first of several entries at the same outline level; must be indirect reference*) Specifies the previous entry in the linked list of outline entries at this level.
Next	dictionary	(*Required if the entry is not the last of several entries at the same outline level; must be indirect reference*) Specifies the next entry in the linked list of outline entries at this level.
First	dictionary	(*Required if an entry has sub-entries; must be indirect reference*) Specifies the outline entry that is the head of the linked list of sub-entries of this outline item.

Last	dictionary	*(Required if an entry has sub-entries; must be indirect reference)* Specifies the outline entry that is the tail of the linked list of sub-entries of this outline item.
Count	integer	*(Required if an entry has sub-entries)* If positive, specifies the number of open descendants the entry has. This includes not just immediate sub-entries, but sub-entries of those entries, and so on. If the value is negative, the entry is closed and the absolute value of **Count** specifies how many entries will appear when the entry is reopened. If an entry has no descendants, the **Count** key should be omitted.

Example 6.8 shows an outline entry. An example of a complete outline tree can be found in Appendix A.

Example 6.8 *Outline entry*

```
22 0 obj
<<
/Parent 21 0 R
/Dest [ 3 0 R /Top 0 792 0 ]
/Title (Document)
/Next 29 0 R
/First 25 0 R
/Last 28 0 R
/Count 4
>>
endobj
```

6.8   Resources

The content of a Page object is represented by a sequence of instructions that produce the text, graphics, and images on that page. The instructions for a particular page may make use of certain objects not contained within that page's description itself but that are either located elsewhere in the PDF file or are PostScript language objects such as fonts. These objects, which are required in order to draw the page but are not stored in the page content itself, are called *resources*.

Resources are not part of a page but are simply referenced by the page. Multiple pages can share a resource. Because resources are stored outside the content of all pages, even pages that share resources remain independent of each other.

PDF currently supports the following resource types: ProcSet, Font, Encoding, FontDescriptor, ColorSpace, and XObject.

Each page includes a list of the ProcSet, Font, and XObject resources it uses. This resource list is stored as a dictionary that is the value of the **Resources** key in the Page object, and has two functions: it enumerates the resources directly needed by the page, and it establishes names by which operators in the page description can refer to the resources. All instructions in the page description that operate on resources refer to them by name.

Each key in the Resources dictionary is a resource type, whose value is a dictionary or an array. If it is a dictionary, it contains keys that are *resource names* and values that are indirect references to the PDF objects specifying the resources. If it is an array, it contains a list of names. Only ProcSet resources are represented as an array in the Resources dictionary; all other resources are represented as dictionaries within the Resources dictionary.

Example 6.9 shows a Resources dictionary containing a ProcSet array, a Font dictionary, and an XObject dictionary. The ProcSet array is described in the following section. The font dictionary contains four fonts named F5, F6, F7, and F8, and associated with object numbers 6, 8, 10, and 12, respectively. The XObject dictionary contains two XObjects named Im1 and Im2 and associated with object numbers 13 and 15, respectively.

Example 6.9 *Resources dictionary*

```
<<
/ProcSet [/PDF /ImageB]
/Font << /F5 6 0 R /F6 8 0 R /F7 10 0 R /F8 12 0 R >>
/XObject << /Im1 13 0 R /Im2 15 0 R >>
>>
```

Some PDF operators take resource names as operands. These resource names are expected to appear in the current page's Resources dictionary. If they do not, an error may be raised or in the case of a font, a default font may be substituted.

6.8.1   ProcSet resources

The types of instructions that may be used in a PDF page description are grouped into independent sets of related instructions. Each of these sets, called procsets, may or may not be used on a particular page. procsets contain implementations of the PDF operators and are used only when a page is printed. The Resources dictionary for each page must contain a **ProcSet** key whose value is an array consisting of the procsets used on that page. Each of the entries in the array must be one of the predefined procsets shown in Table 6.9. The Resources dictionary shown in Example 6.9 contains a **ProcSet** key.

Table 6.9 *Predefined procsets*

Procset Name	Required if the page has any...
PDF	marks on the page whatsoever
Text	text
ImageB	grayscale images or image masks
ImageC	color images
ImageI	indexed images (also called color table images)

6.8.2 Font resources

A PDF font resource is a dictionary specifying the kind of font the resource provides, its real name, its encoding, and information describing the font that can be used to provide a substitute for it when it is not available. A font resource may describe a Type 1 font, an instance of a multiple master Type 1 font, a Type 3 font, or a TrueType font.

All types of fonts supported by PDF share a number of attributes. Table 6.10 lists these attributes.

Table 6.10 *Attributes common to all types of fonts*

Key	Type	Semantics
Type	name	*(Required)* Resource type. Always **Font**.
Name	string	*(Required)* Resource name, used as an operand of the **Tf** operator when selecting the font. **Name** must match the name used in the font dictionary within the page's Resources dictionary.
FirstChar	integer	*(Required except for base 14 Type 1 fonts listed in Table 6.12)* Specifies the first character code defined in the font's **Widths** array.
LastChar	integer	*(Required except for base 14 Type 1 fonts)* Specifies the last character code defined in the font's **Widths** array.

Widths	array	*(Required except for base 14 Type 1 fonts; indirect reference preferred)* An array of **LastChar** – **FirstChar** + 1 widths. For character codes outside the range **FirstChar** to **LastChar**, the value of **MissingWidth** from the font's descriptor is used (see Section 6.8.4, "Font descriptors.") The units in which character widths are measured depend on the type of font resource.
Encoding	name	*(Optional)* Specifies the character encoding of the font. The value of the **Encoding** key may be an encoding resource or the name of a predefined encoding. If this key is not present, the font's built-in encoding is used. Appendix C describes the predefined encodings (**MacRomanEncoding**, **MacExpertEncoding**, and **WinAnsiEncoding**.)

For Type 1 and TrueType fonts, the **BaseFont** key in the font dictionary may contain a *style string*. If the font is a bold, italic, or bold italic font for which no PostScript language name is available, the **BaseFont** key contains the base name of the font with any spaces removed, followed by a comma, followed by a style string. The style string contains one of the strings "Italic", "Bold", or "BoldItalic". For example, the italic variant of the New York font has a **BaseFont** of NewYork,Italic. The PostScript language name of a font is the name which, in a PostScript language program, is used as an operand of the **findfont** operator. It is the name associated with the font by a **definefont** operation. This is usually the value of the **FontName** key in the PostScript language font dictionary of the font. For more information, see Section 5.2 of the *PostScript Language Reference Manual, Second Edition*.

Type1 fonts

Type 1 fonts, described in detail in *Adobe Type 1 Font Format*, are special purpose PostScript language programs used for defining fonts. As compared to Type 3 fonts, Type 1 fonts can be defined more compactly, make use of a special procedure for drawing the characters that results in higher quality output at small sizes and low resolution, and have a built-in mechanism for specifying hints, which are data that indicate basic features of the character shapes not directly expressible by the basic PostScript language operators. In addition, Type 1 fonts that contain a UniqueID in the font itself can be cached across jobs, potentially resulting in enhanced performance. See Section 2.5 of the *Adobe Type 1 Font Format* for further information on UniqueIDs for Type 1 fonts.

Table 6.11 shows the attributes specific to Type 1 font resources.

Note   *Character widths in Type 1 font resources are measured in units in which 1000 units correspond to 1 unit in text space.*

Table 6.11 *Type 1 font attributes*

Key	Type	Semantics
Subtype	name	*(Required)* Type of font. Always **Type1**.
BaseFont	name	*(Required)* PostScript language name or a style string specifying the base font.
FontDescriptor	dictionary	*(Required except for base 14 fonts; must be indirect reference)* A font descriptor resource describing the font's metrics other than its character widths.

Some font attributes can be omitted for the fourteen Type 1 fonts guaranteed to be present with Acrobat Exchange and Acrobat Reader. These fonts are called the base 14 fonts and include members of the Courier, Helvetica˙, and Times˙ families, along with Symbol and ITC Zapf Dingbats. Table 6.12 lists the PostScript language names of these fonts.

Table 6.12 *Base 14 fonts*

Courier	Symbol
Courier-Bold	Times-Roman
Courier-Oblique	Times-Bold
Courier-BoldOblique	Times-Italic
Helvetica	Times-BoldItalic
Helvetica-Bold	ZapfDingbats
Helvetica-Oblique	
Helvetica-BoldOblique	

Example 6.10 shows the font resource for the Adobe Garamond˙ Semibold font. In this example, the font is given the name F1, by which it can be referred to in the PDF page description. The font has an encoding (object number 25), although neither the encoding nor the font descriptor (object number 7) is shown in the example.

Example 6.10 *Type 1 font resource and character widths array*

```
14 0 obj
<<
/Type /Font
/Subtype /Type1
/Name /F1
/BaseFont /AGaramond-Semibold
/Encoding 25 0 R
/FontDescriptor 7 0 R
/FirstChar 0
/LastChar 255
/Widths 21 0 R
>>
endob j
21 0 obj
/Widths [
255 255 255 255 255 255 255 255 255 255 255 255 255 255 255 255 255
255 255 255 255 255 255 255 255 255 255 255 255 255 255 255 255
280 438 510 510 868 834 248 320 320 420 510 255 320 255 347 510
510 510 510 510 510 510 510 510 510 255 255 510 510 510 330 781
627 627 694 784 580 533 743 812 354 354 684 560 921 780 792 588
792 656 504 682 744 650 968 648 590 638 320 329 320 510 500 380
420 510 400 513 409 301 464 522 268 259 484 258 798 533 492 516
503 349 346 321 520 434 684 439 448 390 320 255 320 510 255 627
627 694 580 780 792 744 420 420 420 420 420 420 402 409 409 409
409 268 268 268 268 533 492 492 492 492 492 520 520 520 520 486
400 510 510 506 398 520 555 800 800 1044 360 380 549 846 792 713
510 549 549 510 522 494 713 823 549 274 354 387 768 615 496 330
280 510 549 510 549 612 421 421 1000 255 627 627 792 1016 730 500
1000 438 438 248 248 510 494 448 590 100 510 256 256 539 539 486
255 248 438 1174 627 580 627 580 580 354 354 354 354 792 792 790
792 744 744 744 268 380 380 380 380 380 380 380 380 380 380 ]
endobj
```

Multiple master Type 1 fonts

The multiple master font format is an extension of the Type 1 font format that allows the generation of a wide variety of typeface styles from a single font. This is accomplished through the presence of various design dimensions in the font. Examples of design dimensions are weight (light to extra-bold) and width (condensed to expanded). Coordinates along these design dimensions (such as the degree of boldness) are specified by numbers.

To specify the appearance of the font, numeric values must be supplied for each design dimension of the multiple master font. A completely specified multiple master font is referred to as an *instance* of the multiple master font.

The note *Adobe Type 1 Font Format: Multiple Master Extensions* describes multiple master fonts. An instance of a multiple master font, shown in Table 6.13, has the same keys as an ordinary Type 1 font.

Note   *Character widths in multiple master Type 1 font resources are measured in units in which 1000 units correspond to 1 unit in text space.*

Table 6.13 *Multiple master Type 1 font attributes*

Key	Type	Semantics
Subtype	name	*(Required)* Type of font. Always **MMType1**.
BaseFont	name	*(Required)* Specifies the PostScript language name of the instance. If the name contains spaces (such as "MinionMM 366 465 11"), these spaces are replaced with underscores.
FontDescriptor	dictionary	*(Required; must be indirect reference)* A font descriptor resource describing the font's metrics other than its character widths.

Example 6.11 *Multiple master font resource and character widths array*

```
7 0 obj
<<
/Type /Font
/Subtype /MMType1
/Name /F4
/BaseFont /MinionMM_366_465_11
/FirstChar 32
/LastChar 255
/Widths 19 0 R
/Encoding 5 0 R
/FontDescriptor 6 0 R
>>
endobj
19 0 obj
/Widths [ 187 235 317 430 427 717 607 168 326 326 421 619 219 317 219 282
427 427 427 427 427 427 427 427 427 427 219 219 619 619 619 301
662 568 513 509 593 494 460 558 627 301 296 573 480 753 608 570
489 570 553 428 518 608 584 814 553 526 488 326 279 326 619 500
400 405 462 377 474 386 263 415 471 239 229 446 224 733 484 446
471 461 333 354 275 475 416 607 418 410 367 326 227 326 619 0
567 568 509 493 607 569 607 405 405 405 405 405 405 377 386 386
386 386 239 239 239 239 484 446 446 446 446 446 475 475 475 475
474 324 427 427 472 290 470 482 499 684 672 400 400 0 753 570
0 619 0 0 427 464 0 0 0 0 299 326 0 598 447
301 235 619 0 427 0 0 400 396 991 187 567 567 569 798 664
500 1001 390 391 215 214 619 0 410 526 404 427 245 245 481 480
474 219 215 390 995 567 493 567 493 493 301 301 301 301 569 569
0 569 607 607 607 239 400 400 400 400 253 400 400 400 400 400
]
endobj
```

Type 3 fonts

PostScript Type 3 fonts, also known as user-defined fonts, are described in Section 5.7 of the *PostScript Language Reference Manual, Second Edition.* PDF provides a variant of Type 3 fonts in which characters are defined by streams of PDF page marking operators. These streams, known as CharProcs, are associated with the character names. As with any font, the character names are accessed via an encoding vector.

PDF Type 3 font resources differ from the other font resources provided by PDF. Type 3 font resources define the font itself, while the other font resources simply contain information about the font.

Type 3 fonts are more flexible than Type 1 fonts because the character-drawing streams may contain arbitrary PDF page marking operators. However, Type 3 fonts have no mechanism for improving output at small sizes or low resolutions, and no built-in mechanism for hinting. Table 6.14 shows the attributes specific to Type 3 font resources.

Note   *Character widths and* **FontBBox** *in Type 3 font resources are measured in character space. The transformation from character space to text space is specified by the value of the* **FontMatrix** *key in the Type 3 font dictionary.*

Table 6.14 *Type 3 font attributes*

Key	Type	Semantics
Subtype	name	*(Required)* Type of font. Always **Type3**.
CharProcs	dictionary	*(Required)* Each key in this dictionary is a character name and the value associated with that key is a stream object that draws the character. Any operator that can be used in a PDF page description can be used in this stream. However, the stream must include as its first operator either **d0** (d zero) or **d1**, equivalent to the PostScript language **setcharwidth** and **setcachedevice** operators.
FontBBox	array	*(Required)* Array of four numbers specifying the lower left x, lower left y, upper right x, and upper right y of the font bounding box, in that order. The coordinates are measured in character space. The font bounding box is the smallest rectangle enclosing the shape that results if all characters in the font are placed with their origins coincident, and then painted. **FontBBox** is identical to the PostScript Type 3 font FontBBox.
FontMatrix	array	*(Required)* Specifies the transformation from character space to text space. **FontMatrix** is identical to the PostScript Type 3 font FontMatrix.

Example 6.12 shows a Type 3 font resource.

Example 6.12 *Type 3 font resource*

```
6 0 obj
<<
/Type /Font
/Subtype /Type3
/Name /T36
/CharProcs 1928 0 R
/FontBBox [ −3  −241  875  856 ]
/FontMatrix [ .001 0 0 .001 0 0 ]
/FirstChar 3
/LastChar 101
/Widths 7 0 R
/Encoding 1927 0 R
>>
endobj
7 0 obj
[ 55 0 0 589 0 0 0 0 0 0 0 0 0 0 0 0
0 0 0 0 0 0 0 0 0 0 0 0 0 0 0 0
0 0 0 0 0 31 31 0 0 0 270 0 0 410 40 640
40 0 40 0 40 40 0 0 0 0 0 0 0 0 60 0
58 61 54 52 603 0 29 0 0 853 73 60 62 504 0 659
44 58 60 60 0 0 603 0 0 0 0 0 0 0 0
35 0 35 ]
endobj
```

TrueType fonts

The TrueType font format was developed by Apple Computer. A
TrueType font resource, shown in Table 6.15, has the same keys as a
Type 1 font resource.

Note   *Character widths in TrueType font resources are measured in units in which
1000 units correspond to 1 unit in text space.*

Table 6.15 *TrueType font attributes*

Key	Type	Semantics
Subtype	name	*(Required)* Type of font. Always **TrueType**.
BaseFont	name	*(Required)* Style string specifying the base TrueType font.
FontDescriptor	dictionary	*(Required; must be indirect reference)* A font descriptor resource describing the font's metrics other than its character widths.

Example 6.13 *TrueType font resource*

```
17 0 obj
<<
/Type /Font
/Subtype /TrueType
/Name /F1
/BaseFont /NewYork,Bold
/FirstChar 0
/LastChar 255
/Widths 23 0 R
/Encoding /MacRomanEncoding
/FontDescriptor 7 0 R
>>
endobj
23 0 obj
 [ 0 333 333 333 333 333 333 333 0 333 333 333 333 333 333 333
 333 333 333 333 333 333 333 333 333 333 333 333 0 333 333
 333 303 500 666 666 882 848 303 446 446 507 666 303 378 303 583
 666 666 666 666 666 666 666 666 666 666 303 303 666 666 666 454
 833 757 640 708 810 605 586 772 799 355 461 734 583 973 803 803
 605 803 693 571 704 780 757 1030 651 644 598 409 583 409 666 666
 636 590 670 541 693 571 401 602 696 340 336 625 340 1000 696 636
 689 666 492 484 409 689 613 825 571 636 545 446 246 446 666 333
 757 757 708 605 803 803 780 590 590 590 590 590 590 541 571 571
 571 571 340 340 340 340 696 636 636 636 636 636 689 689 689 689
 666 325 666 666 666 666 666 647 886 886 894 636 636 666 1011 803
 666 666 666 666 666 670 651 636 799 757 534 363 390 886 894 636
 454 303 666 894 666 666 803 541 541 1030 666 757 757 803 1113 1015
 515 1030 530 530 303 303 666 666 636 644 98 659 321 321 689 696
 666 666 303 530 1280 757 605 757 605 605 355 355 355 355 803 803
 790 803 780 780 780 340 636 636 636 636 636 636 636 636 636 636
 ]
endobj
```

6.8.3 Encoding resources

An encoding resource describes a font's character encoding, the mapping between numeric character codes and character names. These character names are keys in the font dictionary and are used to retrieve the code which draws the character. Thus, the font encoding provides the link which associates numeric character codes with the glyphs drawn when those codes are encountered in text. An encoding resource is a dictionary whose contents are shown in Table 6.16.

Table 6.16 *Font encoding attributes*

Key	Type	Semantics
BaseEncoding	name	*(Optional)* Specifies the encoding from which the new encoding differs. This key is not present if the encoding is based on the base font's encoding. Otherwise it must be one of the predefined encodings **MacRomanEncoding**, **MacExpertEncoding**, or **WinAnsiEncoding**, described in Appendix C.
Differences	array	*(Optional)* Describes the differences from the base encoding.

The value of the **Differences** key is an array of character codes and glyph names organized as follows:

$$\text{code}_1 \text{ /name}_{11} \text{ /name}_{12} \ldots \text{ /name}_{1i}$$
$$\text{code}_2 \text{ /name}_{21} \text{ /name}_{22} \ldots \text{ /name}_{1j}$$
$$\ldots$$
$$\text{code}_n \text{ /name}_{n1} \text{ /name}_{n2} \ldots \text{ /name}_{nk}$$

Each code is the first index in a sequence of characters to be changed. The first glyph name after the code becomes the name corresponding to that code. Subsequent names replace consecutive code indexes until the next code appears in the array or the array ends.

For example, in the encoding in Example 6.14, the glyph quotesingle (') is associated with character code 39. Adieresis (Ä) is associated with code 128, Aring (Å) with 129, and trademark (™) with 170.

Example 6.14 *Font encoding*

```
25 0 obj
<<
/Type /Encoding
/Differences [ 39 /quotesingle 96 /grave 128 /Adieresis /Aring /Ccedilla /Eacute
/Ntilde /Odieresis /Udieresis /aacute /agrave /acircumflex /adieresis
/atilde /aring /ccedilla /eacute /egrave /ecircumflex /edieresis
/iacute /igrave /icircumflex /idieresis /ntilde /oacute /ograve
/ocircumflex /odieresis /otilde /uacute /ugrave /ucircumflex /udieresis
/dagger /degree /cent /sterling /section /bullet /paragraph /germandbls
/registered /copyright /trademark /acute /dieresis 174 /AE /Oslash
177 /plusminus 180 /yen /mu 187 /ordfeminine /ordmasculine 190 /ae
/oslash /questiondown /exclamdown /logicalnot 196 /florin 199 /guillemotleft
/guillemotright /ellipsis 203 /Agrave /Atilde /Otilde /OE /oe /endash
/emdash /quotedblleft /quotedblright /quoteleft /quoteright /divide
216 /ydieresis /Ydieresis /fraction /currency /guilsinglleft /guilsinglright
/fi /fl /daggerdbl /periodcentered /quotesinglbase /quotedblbase
/perthousand /Acircumflex /Ecircumflex /Aacute /Edieresis /Egrave
/Iacute /Icircumflex /Idieresis /Igrave /Oacute /Ocircumflex 241
/Ograve /Uacute /Ucircumflex /Ugrave /dotlessi /circumflex /tilde
/macron /breve /dotaccent /ring /cedilla /hungarumlaut /ogonek /caron ]
>>
endobj
```

6.8.4 Font descriptors

A font descriptor specifies a font's metrics, attributes, and glyphs. These metrics provide information needed to create a substitute multiple master font when the original font is unavailable. The font descriptor may also be used to embed the original font in the PDF file.

A font descriptor is a dictionary, as shown in Table 6.17, whose keys specify various font attributes. Most keys are similar to the keys found in Type 1 font and FontInfo dictionaries described in Section 5.2 of the *PostScript Language Reference Manual, Second Edition* and the *Adobe Type 1 Font Format*. All integer values are units in character space. The conversion from character space to text space depends on the type of font. See the discussion in Section 6.8.2, "Font resources."

Note   *For detailed information on the coordinate system in which characters are defined, see Section 5.4 in the* PostScript Language Reference Manual, Second Edition *or Section 3.1 in the* Adobe Type 1 Font Format.

Table 6.17 *Font descriptor attributes*

Key	Type	Semantics
Type	name	(*Required*) Resource type. Always **FontDescriptor**.
Ascent	integer	(*Required*) The maximum height above the baseline reached by characters in this font, excluding the height of accented characters.
CapHeight	integer	(*Required*) The y-coordinate of the top of flat capital letters, measured from the baseline.
Descent	integer	(*Required*) The maximum depth below the baseline reached by characters in this font. **Descent** is a negative number.
Flags	integer	(*Required*) Collection of flags defining various characteristics of the font. See Table 6.19.
FontBBox	array	(*Required*) Array of four numbers specifying the lower left x, lower left y, upper right x, and upper right y of the font bounding box, in that order. The font bounding box is the smallest rectangle enclosing the shape that results if all characters in the font are placed with their origins coincident, and then painted.
FontName	name	(*Required*) The name passed to the PostScript language **definefont** operator.
ItalicAngle	integer	(*Required*) Angle in degrees counterclockwise from the vertical of the dominant vertical strokes of the font. **ItalicAngle** is negative for fonts that slope to the right, as almost all italic fonts do.
StemV	integer	(*Required*) The width of vertical stems in characters.
AvgWidth	integer	(*Optional*) The average width of characters in this font. The default value is 0.
FontFile	stream	(*Optional*) A complete Type 1 font definition.

Leading	integer	(*Optional*) The desired spacing between lines of text. The default value is 0.
MaxWidth	integer	(*Optional*) The maximum width of characters in this font. The default value is 0.
MissingWidth	integer	(*Optional*) The width to use for unencoded character codes. The default value is 0.
StemH	integer	(*Optional*) The width of horizontal stems in characters. The default value is 0.
XHeight	integer	(*Optional*) The *y*-coordinate of the top of flat non-ascending lowercase letters, measured from the baseline. The default value is 0.

Font files

Currently, a multiple master Type 1 font can only be used to substitute for fonts that use the Adobe Roman Standard Character Set as defined in Appendix E.5 of the *PostScript Language Reference Manual, Second Edition*. To make a document portable, it is necessary to embed fonts that do not use this character set. The only exceptions are the fonts Symbol and ITC Zapf Dingbats, which are assumed to be present.

Currently, only Type 1 fonts may be embedded in a PDF file. They are embedded using the FontFile mechanism. The value of the **FontFile** key in a font descriptor is a stream that contains a Type 1 font definition. A Type 1 font definition, as described in the *Adobe Type 1 Font Format*, consists of three parts: a clear text portion, an encrypted portion, and a fixed content portion. The fixed content portion contains 512 ASCII zeros followed by a **cleartomark** operator, and perhaps followed by additional data. The stream dictionary for a font file contains the standard **Length** and **Filter** keys plus the additional keys shown in Table 6.18. While the encrypted portion of a Type 1 font may be in binary or ASCII hexadecimal format, PDF only supports binary format. Because the stream containing the Type 1 font data contains binary data, the stream must be converted to ASCII using either ASCII hexadecimal or ASCII base-85 encoding. Example 6.15 shows the structure of an embedded Type 1 font.

Table 6.18 *Additional attributes for FontFile stream*

Key	Type	Semantics
Length1	integer	(*Required*) Length in bytes of the ASCII portion of the Type 1 font file after it has been decoded using the filters specified by the stream's **Filter** key.
Length2	integer	(*Required*) Length in bytes of the encrypted portion of the Type 1 font file after it has been decoded using the filters specified by the stream's **Filter** key.
Length3	integer	(*Required*) Length in bytes of the portion of the Type 1 font file that contains the 512 zeroes, plus the **cleartomark** operator, plus any following data. This is the length of the data after it has been decoded using the filters specified by the stream's **Filter** key. If **Length3** is zero, it indicates that the 512 zeroes and **cleartomark** have not been included in the **FontFile** and must be added.

Example 6.15 *Embedded Type 1 font definition*

```
12 0 obj
<<
/Filter /ASCII85Decode
/Length 13 0 R
/Length1 15 0 R
/Length2 14 0 R
/Length3 16 0 R
>>
stream
,p>`rDKJj'E+LaU0eP.@+AH9dBOu$hFD55nCf"gt<-N7'0b#in+Co1rF<G%(B5)5m
… omitted data …
9J*:(%q07k&$"[V@rJJQ&Nt')<=^p&mGf(%:%h1%9c//K(/*o=.C>UXkbVGTrr~>
endstream
endobj
13 0 obj
41116
endobj
14 0 obj
32393
endobj
15 0 obj
2526
endobj
16 0 obj
570
endobj
```

Flags

The value of the flags key in a font descriptor is a 32-bit integer that contains a collection of boolean attributes. These attributes are *true* if the corresponding bit is set in the integer. Table 6.19 specifies the meanings of the bits, with bit 1 being the least significant. Reserved bits must be set to zero.

Table 6.19 *Font flags*

Bit position	Semantics
1	Fixed-width font
2	Serif font
3	Symbolic font
4	Script font
5	Reserved
6	Uses Adobe standard encoding
7	Italic
8–16	Reserved
17	All cap font
18	Small cap font
19	Force bold at small text sizes
20–32	Reserved

All characters in a fixed-width font have the same width, while characters in a proportional font have different widths. Characters in a serif font have short strokes drawn at an angle on the top and bottom of character stems, while sans serif fonts do not have such strokes. A symbolic font contains symbols rather than letters and numbers. Characters in a script font resemble cursive handwriting. An all cap font, which is typically used for display purposes such as titles or headlines, contains no lowercase letters. It differs from a small cap font in that characters in the latter, while also capital letters, have been sized and their proportions adjusted so that they have the same size and stroke weight as lowercase characters in the same typeface family. Figure 6.3 shows examples of these types of fonts.

Figure 6.3 *Characteristics represented in the flags field of a font descriptor*

The quick brown fox jumped...	Fixed-width font
The quick brown fox jumped...	Sans serif font
The quick brown fox jumped...	Serif font
▼♠❷⓪❷①✳✻❶⑦❷❾☙③◆⑤	Symbolic font
The quick brown fox jumped...	Script font
The quick brown fox jumped...	Italic font
THE QUICK BROWN FOX JUMPED...	All cap font

Bit 6 in the flags field indicates whether the font's built-in encoding is Adobe standard encoding, described in Appendix C. Finally, bit 19 is used to determine whether or not bold characters are drawn with extra pixels even at very small text sizes. Typically, when characters are drawn at small sizes on very low resolution devices such as display screens, features of bold characters may appear only one pixel wide. Because this is the minimum feature width on a pixel-based device, ordinary non-bold characters also appear with one-pixel wide features, and cannot be distinguished from bold characters. If the force bold bit is set, features of bold characters may be thickened at small text sizes.

Example 6.16 *Font descriptor*

```
7 0 obj
<<
/Type /FontDescriptor
/FontName /AGaramond-Semibold
/Flags 262192
/FontBBox [ -177 -269 1123 866 ]
/MissingWidth 255
/StemV 105
/StemH 45
/CapHeight 660
/XHeight 394
/Ascent 720
/Descent -270
/Leading 83
/MaxWidth 1212
/AvgWidth 478
/ItalicAngle 0
>>
endobj
```

6.8.5 Color space resources

A color space specifies how color values should be interpreted. While some PDF operators implicitly specify the color space they use, others such as image objects require a color space to be specified. PDF supports four types of color spaces: **DeviceGray**, **DeviceRGB**, **DeviceCMYK**, and indexed. The color spaces follow the semantics described in Section 4.8 of the *PostScript Language Reference Manual, Second Edition.*

All the color spaces supported by PDF are device color spaces, not device-independent color spaces. This means that the exact color produced depends on the characteristics of the output device. For example, in the DeviceRGB color space, a value of 1 for the red component means "turn red all the way on." If the output device is a monitor, the color displayed depends strongly on the settings of the monitor's brightness, contrast, and color balance adjustments. In addition, the precise color displayed depends on the chemical composition of the compound used as the red phosphor in the particular monitor being used, the length of time the monitor has been turned on, and the age of the monitor.

Colors in the **DeviceGray** color space are specified by a single value— the intensity of achromatic light. In this color space, 0 is black, 1 is white, and intermediate values represent shades of gray.

Colors in the **DeviceRGB** color space are represented by three values: the intensity of the red, green, and blue components in the output. **DeviceRGB** is commonly used for video displays because they are generally based on red, green, and blue phosphors.

Colors in the **DeviceCMYK** color space are represented by four values. These values are the amounts of the cyan, magenta, yellow, and black components in the output. This color space is commonly used for color printers, where they are the colors of the inks traditionally used for four-color printing. Only cyan, magenta, and yellow are strictly necessary, but black is generally also used in printing because black ink produces a better black than a mixture of cyan, magenta, and yellow inks, and because black ink is less expensive than the other inks.

Indexed color spaces allow colors to be specified by small integers that are used as indexes into a table of color values. The values in this table are colors specified in either the **DeviceRGB** or **DeviceCMYK** color space. For example, an indexed color space can have white as color number 1, dark blue as color number 2, turquoise as color number 3, and black as color number 4.

An indexed color space is specified as follows:

[/Indexed *base hival lookup*]

The base color space is specified by *base* and must be either **DeviceRGB** or **DeviceCMYK**. The maximum valid index value, specified by *hival*, is determined by the number of colors desired in the indexed color space. Colors will be specified by integers in the range 0 to *hival*. The color table values are contained in *lookup*, which is a PDF stream. The stream contains $m \times (hival + 1)$ bytes where *m* is the number of color components in the base color space. Each byte is an unsigned integer in the range 0 to 255 that is divided by 255, yielding a color component value in the range 0 to 1. The color components for each entry in the table are adjacent in the stream. For example, if the base color space is DeviceRGB and the indexed color space contains two colors, the order of bytes in the stream is: R0 G0 B0 R1 G1 B1, where letters are the color component and numbers are the table entry.

A color space is specified either by a name or an array. If a name is used, it must be **DeviceGray**, **DeviceRGB**, or **DeviceCMYK**. If an array is used, it can contain one of the color space names or specify an indexed color space.

Example 6.17 shows a color space resource for an indexed color space. Colors in the table are specified in the **DeviceRGB** color space, and the table contains 256 entries. The stream containing the table has been LZW and ASCII base-85 encoded.

Example 6.17 *Color space resource for an indexed color space*

```
12 0 obj
[ /Indexed /DeviceRGB 255 13 0 R ]
endobj
13 0 obj
<< /Filter [ /ASCII85Decode /LZWDecode ] /Length 554 >>
stream
J3Vsg-=dE=!]*)rE$,8^$P%cp+RI0B1)A)g_;FLE.V90YKVi0lQu")JAqHGDk%l>T
(1r<<hr?[Ec42X`N8\8+Cc21lJq,!%#Y5"4!2)V%&\1TdK$9&#.M9au6>79n6`Q:4
PbLSZTLEE(8E@'*1mg_*eTnN*;*'V3+gm-EEetX%;Bo$ur2ss*N`.-!.kG_q6GDD'
dKoL!8Ka#EV,@V!\j8ZFbp6EE<9cn=N6j<M8Q?[#7"dq'1>0nf;(&;QU6bUD')c@\
9-d\DA=cZ0Q>glM$$;cd2O@&a;X,Nn_a<?V-PVE%?Sf]idH6WRZqHGq]Zm<uCi"]?
Stg(<gV-H9NB<SA\T=sN)ll%(BDIak7/H&mV!kmDUo4X;8;]V>P(Jl1aRc(K1^ue>
gF/(+GaKo$qneLWDrQ#;5\S(\$q':Lrd;ZiPZ2fpLFc\K`Wj@lBh!h^Cgom<oQ4<X
KoCCZ8-L8l:<8*qN(?MC9U%ibKB/Oa8csl:1s1FbX=_TsXL'?JJjd6obQ6M;)GG]u
bS/5%"OmlTJ]=PC!c2]]^rh(A~>
endstream
endobj
```

6.8.6 XObject resources

XObjects are named resources that appear in the XObject subdictionary within the Resources dictionary of a page object. PDF currently supports two types of XObjects: images and forms. In the future it may support other object types such as sound and video.

XObjects are passed by name to the **Do** operator, described in Section 7.8, "XObject operator." The action taken by the **Do** operator depends on the type of XObject passed to it. In the case of images and forms, the **Do** operator draws the XObject.

Image resources

An image resource is an XObject whose **Subtype** is **Image**. Image resources allow a PDF page description to specify a sampled image or image mask. PDF supports image masks, 1-, 2-, 4-, and 8-bit grayscale images, and 1-, 2-, 4-, and 8-bit per component color images. Color images may have three or four components representing either RGB or CMYK.

The sample data format and sample interpretation conform to the conventions required by the PostScript language **image** and **imagemask** operators. However, all PDF images have a size of 1×1 unit in user space, and the data must be specified left-to-right, top-to-bottom. Like images in the PostScript language, PDF images are sized and positioned by adjusting the current transformation matrix in the page description.

An image resource is specified by a stream object. Like all PDF streams, the image data must be encoded in ASCII. The stream dictionary must include the standard keys required of all streams as well as additional ones described in the following table. Several of the keys are the same as those required by the PostScript language **image** and **imagemask** operators. Matching keys have the same semantics.

Table 6.20 *Image attributes*

Key	Type	Semantics
Type	name	(*Required*) Resource type. Always **XObject**.
Subtype	name	(*Required*) Resource subtype. Always **Image**.
Name	name	(*Required*) Resource name, used as an operand of the **Do** operator. **Name** must match the name used in the XObject dictionary within the page's Resources dictionary.
Width	integer	(*Required*) Width of the source image in samples.
Height	integer	(*Required*) Height of the source image in samples.
BitsPerComponent	integer	(*Required*) The number of bits used to represent each color component.
ColorSpace	color space	(*Required for images, not allowed for image masks*) Color space used for the image samples.
Decode	array	(*Optional*) An array of numbers specifying the mapping from sample values in the image to values appropriate for the current color space. The number of elements in the array must be twice the number of color components in the color space specified in the **ColorSpace** key. The default value results in the image sample values being used directly. The **Decode** array is described further in the text.
Interpolate	boolean	(*Optional*) If *true*, requests that image interpolation be performed. Interpolation attempts to smooth transitions between sample values. Interpolation may be performed differently by different devices, and not at all by some. The default value is *false*.
ImageMask	boolean	(*Optional*) Specifies whether the image should be treated as a mask. If *true*, the image is treated as a mask; **BitsPerComponent** must be 1, **ColorSpace** should not be provided, and the mask is drawn using the current fill color. If *false*, the image is not treated as a mask. The default value is *false*.

Example 6.18 shows an image object. It is a monochrome (1-bit per component, **DeviceGray**) image that is 24 samples wide and 23 samples high. Interpolation is not requested and the default decode array is used. The image is given the name Im0, which is used to refer to the image when it is drawn.

Example 6.18 *Image resource with length specified as an indirect object*

```
5 0 obj
<<
/Type /XObject
/Subtype /Image
/Name /Im0
/Width 24
/Height 23
/BitsPerComponent 1
/ColorSpace /DeviceGray
/Filter /ASCIIHexDecode
/Length 6 0 R
>>
stream
 003B00 002700 002480 0E4940
 114920 14B220 3CB650 75FE88
 17FF8C 175F14 1C07E2 3803C4
 703182 F8EDFC B2BBC2 BB6F84
 31BFC2 18EA3C 0E3E00 07FC00
 03F800 1E1800 1FF800>
endstream
endobj
6 0 obj
174
endobj
```

The **Decode** array can be used to invert the colors in an image or to compress or expand the range of values specified in the image data. Each pair of numbers in the **Decode** array specifies the upper and lower values to which the range of sample values in the image is mapped. The **Decode** array contains one pair of numbers for each component in the color space specified in the image. The mapping for each color component is a linear mapping that, for a **Decode** array of the form $[D_{Min}\ D_{Max}]$, can be written as:

$$o = D_{Min} + i \times \frac{D_{Max} - D_{Min}}{2^n - 1}$$

where:

n is the value of **BitsPerComponent**
i is the input value, in the range 0 to $2^n - 1$
D_{Min} and D_{Max} are the values specified in the **Decode** array
o is the output value, to be interpreted in the color space of the image.

Samples with a value of zero are mapped to D_{Min}, samples with a value of $2^n - 1$ are mapped to D_{Max}, and samples with intermediate values are mapped linearly between D_{Min} and D_{Max}. The default **Decode** array for each color component is [0 1], causing sample values in the range 0 to $2^n - 1$ to be mapped to color values in the range 0 to 1. Table 6.21 shows the default **Decode** arrays for various color spaces.

Table 6.21 *Default **Decode** arrays for various color spaces*

Color space	Default decode array
DeviceGray	[0 1]
DeviceRGB	[0 1 0 1 0 1]
DeviceCMYK	[0 1 0 1 0 1 0 1]
Indexed	[0 N] where N = $2^n - 1$

As an example of the **Decode** array, consider a **DeviceGray** image with 8 bits per component. The color of each sample in a **DeviceGray** image is represented by a single number. The default **Decode** array maps a sample value of 0 to a color value of 0 and a sample value of 255 to a color value of 1. A negative image is produced by specifying a **Decode** array of [1 0], which maps a sample value of 0 to a color value of 1 and a sample value of 255 maps to a color value of 0. If the image only contains values from 0 to 63 and is to be displayed using the full gray range of 0 to 1, a decode array of [0 4] should be used. With this **Decode** array, a sample value of 0 maps to a color value of 0, a sample value of 255 maps to a color value of 4, and a sample value of 63 (the maximum value in the example) maps to a color value of 0.99.

Form resources

A form is a self-contained description of any text, graphics, or sampled images that is drawn multiple times on several pages or at different locations on a single page.

A Form resource is specified by a PDF stream. The keys in the stream dictionary correspond to the keys in a PostScript language Form dictionary. Unlike a PostScript language Form dictionary, the Form resource dictionary does not contain a **PaintProc** key. Instead, the stream contents specify the painting procedure. These contents must be described using the same marking operators that are used for PDF page descriptions. As usual, the stream must also include a **Length** key and may include **Filter** and **DecodeParms** keys if the stream is encoded. Table 6.22 describes the attributes of a Form resource dictionary.

To draw a form, the **Do** operator is used, with the name of the form to be drawn given as an operand. As discussed in the introduction to Section 6.8, "Resources," this name is mapped to an object ID using the Resources dictionary for the page on which the form is drawn.

Table 6.22 *Form attributes*

Key	Type	Semantics
Type	name	(*Required*) Resource type. Always **XObject**.
Subtype	name	(*Required*) Resource subtype. Always **Form**.
BBox	array	(*Required*) An array of four numbers that specifies the form's bounding box in the form coordinate system. This bounding box is used to clip the output of the form and to determine its size for caching.
FormType	integer	(*Required*) Must be 1.
Matrix	matrix	(*Required*) A transformation matrix that maps from the form's coordinate space into user space.
Name	name	(*Required*) Resource name, used as an operand of the **Do** operator. **Name** must match the name used in the XObject dictionary within the page's Resources dictionary.
Resources	dictionary	(*Optional*) A list of the resources such as fonts and images required by this form. The dictionary's format is the same as for the Resources dictionary in a Page object. All resources used in the form must be included in the Resources dictionary of the Page object on which the form appears, regardless of whether or not they also appear in the Resources dictionary of the form. It can be useful to also specify them in the Form's Resources dictionary in order to easily determine which resources are used inside the form. If a resource is included in both the Form's **Resources** and the Resources dictionary for the page, it should have the same name in both locations.
XUID	array	(*Optional*) An ID that uniquely identifies the form. This allows the form to be cached after the first time it has been drawn in order to improve the speed of subsequent redraws.

XUID arrays may contain any number of elements. The first element in an **XUID** array is the organization ID. Forms that are used only in closed environments may use 1000000 as the organization ID. Any value can be used for subsequent elements, but the same values must not be used for different forms. Organizations that plan to distribute forms widely and wish to use XUIDs must obtain an organization ID from Adobe Systems Incorporated, as described in Appendix E. Section 5.8 of the *PostScript Language Reference Manual, Second Edition* provides a further explanation of XUIDs.

Example 6.19 *Form resource*

```
6 0 obj
<<
/Type /XObject
/Subtype /Form
/Name /Fm0
/FormType 1
/BBox [ 0 0 1000 1000 ]
/Matrix [ 1 0 0 1 0 0 ]
/Length 38
>>
stream
 0 0 m 0 1000 l 1000 1000 l 1000 0 l f
endstream
endobj
```

6.9   Info dictionary

A PDF document typically includes the information shown in Table 6.23 in the Info dictionary. None of the keys in the Info dictionary is required. The characters in the strings contained in the Info dictionary are encoded using the predefined encoding **PDFDocEncoding**, described in Appendix C.

Note   *Omit any key in the Info dictionary for which a value is not known, rather than including it with an empty string as its value.*

Table 6.23 *PDF Info dictionary attributes*

Key	Type	Semantics
Author	string	*(Optional)* The name of the person who created the document.
CreationDate	string	*(Optional)* The date the document was created. It should be stored in an unambiguous format. For example, 11 October 1992 13:11 is preferable to 11/10/92 1:11 pm. The date should be in the same language as the document content.
Creator	string	*(Optional)* If the document was converted into a PDF document from another form, the name of the application that created the original document.
Producer	string	*(Optional)* The name of the application that converted the document from its native format to PDF.

Example 6.20 shows an example of an Info dictionary.

Example 6.20 *Info dictionary*

```
1 0 obj
<<
/Creator (Adobe Illustrator)
/CreationDate (Thursday Feb 04 08:06:03 1993)
/Author (Werner Heisenberg)
/Producer (Acrobat Network Distiller 1.0 for Macintosh)
>>
endobj
```

CHAPTER 7

Page Descriptions

This chapter describes the PDF operators that draw text, graphics, and images on the page. It completes the specification of PDF. The following chapters describe how to produce efficient PDF files.

Text, graphics, and images are drawn using the coordinate systems described in Chapter 3. It may be useful to refer to that chapter when reading the description of various operators, to obtain a better understanding of the coordinate systems used in PDF documents and the relationships among them.

Appendix B contains a complete list of operators, arranged alphabetically.

Note   *Throughout this chapter, PDF operators are shown with a list of the operands they require. A dash (—) is used to indicate that an operator takes no operands. In addition, for operators that correspond to one or more PostScript language operators, the corresponding PostScript language operators appear in bold on the first line of the operator's definition. An operand specified as a number may be either integer or real. Otherwise, numeric operands must be integer.*

7.1   Overview

A PDF page description can be considered a sequence of graphics objects. These objects generate marks that are applied to the current page, obscuring any previous marks they may overlay.

PDF provides four types of graphics objects:

- A path object is an arbitrary shape made of straight lines, rectangles, and cubic curves. A path may intersect itself and may have disconnected sections and holes. A path object includes a painting operator that specifies whether the path is filled, is stroked, and/or serves as a clipping path.

- A text object consists of one or more character strings that can be placed anywhere on the page and in any orientation. Like a path, text can be stroked, filled, and/or serve as a clipping path.

- An image object consists of a set of samples using a specified color model. Images can be placed anywhere on a page and in any orientation.

- An XObject is a PDF object referenced by name. The interpretation of an XObject depends on its type. PDF currently supports two types of XObjects: images and PostScript language forms.

As described in Section 6.8, "Resources," a PDF page description is not necessarily self-contained. It often contains references to resources such as fonts, forms, or images not found within the page description itself but located elsewhere in the PDF file.

7.2   Graphics state

The exact effect of drawing a graphics or text object is determined by parameters such as the current line thickness, font, and leading. These parameters are part of the *graphics state*.

Although the contents of the PDF graphics state are similar to those of the graphics state in the PostScript language, PDF extends the graphics state to include separate stroke and fill colors and additional elements that affect only text. The use of separate fill and stroke colors in PDF is necessary to implement painting operators that both fill and stroke a path or text. The additional text state enables the implementation of a more compact set of text operators.

Tables 7.1 and 7.2 list the parameters in the graphics state, arranged alphabetically. For each parameter, the table lists the operator that sets the parameter, along with any restriction on where the operator may appear in a page description. For convenience, the text-specific elements are listed separately.

Note   *None of the graphics state operators may appear within a path.*

Table 7.1 *General graphics state parameters*

Parameter	Operator	Operator may not appear...
clipping path		*see the description of the clipping path in Section 7.2.1, "Clipping path"*
CTM	**cm**	within a text object or path
current point		*see the description of the current point in Section 7.2.3, "Current point"*
fill color	**g, rg, k**	within a path
flatness	**i**	within a path
line cap style	**J**	within a path
line dash pattern	**d**	within a path
line join style	**j**	within a path
line width	**w**	within a path
miter limit	**M**	within a path
stroke color	**G, RG, K**	within a path

Table 7.2 *Text-specific graphics state parameters*

Parameter	Operator	Operator may not appear...
character spacing	**Tc**	within a path
	"	outside a text object
horizontal scaling	**Tz**	within a path
leading	**TL**	within a path
	TD	outside a text object
text font	**Tf**	within a path
text matrix	**Tm**	outside of a text object
text rise	**Ts**	within a path
text size	**Tf**	within a path
text rendering mode	**Tr**	within a path
word spacing	**Tw**	within a path
	"	outside a text object

The graphics state is initialized at the beginning of each page, using the default values specified in each of the graphics state operator descriptions.

PDF provides a graphics state stack for saving and restoring the graphics state. PDF provides an operator that saves a copy of the entire graphics state onto the graphics state stack. Another operator removes the most recently saved graphics state from the stack and makes it the current graphics state.

Each of the elements in Table 7.1 is described in the following sections, while the operators that set these parameters are described in Section 7.3, "Graphics state operators" and Section 7.4, "Color operators." The text-specific parameters listed in Table 7.2 are described in Section 7.6, "Text state," near the discussion of text objects. The operators that set them are described in Sections 7.7.2, "Text state operators" and 7.7.3, "Text positioning operators."

7.2.1 Clipping path

The clipping path restricts the region to which paint can be applied on a page. Marks outside the region bounded by the clipping path are not painted. Clipping paths may be specified either by a path, or by using one of the clipping modes for text rendering. These are described in Sections 7.5.3, "Path clipping operators" and 7.6.6, "Text rendering mode."

7.2.2 CTM

The CTM is the matrix specifying the transformation from user space to device space. It is described in Section 3.2, "User space."

7.2.3 Current point

All drawing on a page makes use of the *current point*. In an analogy to drawing on paper, the current point can be thought of as the location of the pen used for drawing.

The current point must be set before graphics can be drawn on a page. Several of the operators discussed in Section 7.5.1, "Path segment operators" set the current point. As a path object is constructed, the current point is updated in the same way as a pen moves when drawing graphics on a piece of paper. After the path is painted using the operators described in Section 7.5.2, "Path painting operators," the current point is undefined.

The current point also determines where text is drawn. Each time a text object begins, the current point is set to the origin of the page's coordinate system. Several of the operators described in Section 7.7.3, "Text positioning operators" change the current point. The current point is also updated as text is drawn using the operators described in 7.7.4, "Text string operators."

7.2.4 Fill color

The fill color is used to paint the interior of paths and text characters that are filled. Filling is described in Section 7.5.2, "Path painting operators."

7.2.5 Flatness

Flatness sets the maximum permitted distance in device pixels between the mathematically correct path and an approximation constructed from straight line segments, as shown in Figure 7.1.

Note   *Flatness is inherently device-dependent, because it is measured in device pixels.*

Figure 7.1 *Flatness*

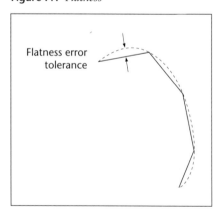

7.2.6 Line cap style

The line cap style specifies the shape to be used at the ends of open subpaths when they are stroked. Allowed values are shown in Figure 7.2.

Figure 7.2 *Line cap styles*

	Line cap style	Description
	0	Butt end caps—the stroke is squared off at the endpoint of the path.
	1	Round end caps—a semicircular arc with a diameter equal to the line width is drawn around the endpoint and filled in.
	2	Projecting square end caps—the stroke extends beyond the end of the line by a distance which is half the line width and is squared off.

7.2.7 Line dash pattern

The line dash pattern controls the pattern of dashes and gaps used to stroke paths. It is specified by an array and a phase. The array specifies the length of alternating dashes and gaps. The phase specifies the distance into the dash pattern to start the dash. Both the elements of the array and the phase are measured in user space units. Before beginning to stroke a path, the array is cycled through, adding up the lengths of dashes and gaps. When the sum of dashes and gaps equals the value specified by the phase, stroking of the path begins, using the array from the point that has been reached. Figure 7.3 shows examples of line dash patterns. As can be seen from the figure, the command **[ ] 0 d** can be used to restore the dash pattern to a solid line.

Figure 7.3 *Line dash pattern*

Dash pattern	Array and phase	Description
	[ ] 0	Turn dash off–solid line
	[3] 0	3 units on, 3 units off, …
	[2] 1	1 on, 2 off, 2 on, 2 off, …
	[2 1] 0	2 on, 1 off, 2 on, 1 off, …
	[3 5] 6	2 off, 3 on, 5 off, 3 on, 5 off, …
	[2 3] 11	1 on, 3 off, 2 on, 3 off, 2 on, …

Dashed lines wrap around curves and corners just as solid stroked lines do. The ends of each dash are treated with the current line cap style, and corners within dashes are treated with the current line join style.

7.2.8 Line join style

The line join style specifies the shape to be used at the corners of paths that are stroked. Figure 7.4 shows the allowed values.

Figure 7.4 *Line join styles*

	Line join style	Description
	0	Miter joins —the outer edges of the strokes for the two segments are continued until they meet. If the extension projects too far, as determined by the miter limit, a bevel join is used instead.
	1	Round joins—a circular arc with a diameter equal to the line width is drawn around the point where the segments meet and filled in, producing a rounded corner.
	2	Bevel joins—the two path segments are drawn with butt end caps (see the discussion of line cap style), and the resulting notch beyond the ends of the segments is filled in with a triangle.

7.2.9 Line width

The line width specifies the thickness of the line used to stroke a path and is measured in user space units. A line width of 0 specifies that the line be the thinnest line that can be rendered on the output device.

Note   *A line width of 0 is an inherently device-dependent value. Its use is discouraged because the line may be nearly invisible when printing on high-resolution devices.*

7.2.10 Miter limit

When two line segments meet at a sharp angle and mitered joins have been specified as the line join style, it is possible for the miter to extend far beyond the thickness of the line stroking the path. The miter limit imposes a limit on the ratio of the miter length to the line width, as shown in Figure 7.5. When the limit is exceeded, the join is converted from a miter to a bevel join. Examples of miter limit values are: 1.415 converts to bevels for φ less than 90 degrees, 2.0 converts to bevels for φ less than 60 degrees, and 10.0 converts to bevels for φ less than 11 degrees.

Figure 7.5 *Miter length*

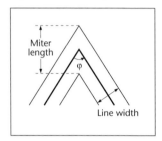

7.2.11 Stroke color

The stroke color is used to paint the border of paths and text that are stroked. Stroking is described in Section 7.5.2, "Path painting operators."

7.3 Graphics state operators

PDF provides operators to set each of the graphics state parameters described in Section 7.2, "Graphics state." This section describes all the operators used to set all the parameters shown in Table 7.1 except clipping path, current point, and stroke and fill color. Stroke and fill color are described in the following section.

None of the graphics state operators described in this section can be used within a path object. All except those that save and restore the graphics state (**q** and **Q**) or set the CTM (**cm**) can be included within text objects.

— **q** Saves the current graphics state on the graphics state stack.

— **Q**   Restores the graphics state to the most recently saved state. Removes the most recently saved state from the stack and makes it the current state.

a b c d e f **cm**   **concat**
Modifies the CTM by concatenating the specified matrix. Although the operands specify a matrix, they are passed as six numbers, not an array.

[array] phase **d**   **setdash**
Sets the dash pattern parameter in the graphics state. If *array* is empty, the dash pattern is a solid, unbroken line, otherwise *array* is an array of numbers, all non-negative and at least one non-zero, that specifies distances in user space for the length of dashes and gaps. *phase* is a number that specifies a distance in user space into the dash pattern at which to begin marking the path. The default dash pattern is a solid line.

flatness **i**   **setflat**
Sets the flatness parameter in the graphics state. *flatness* is a number in the range 0 to 100, inclusive. The default value for *flatness* is 0, which means that the device's default flatness is used.

linejoin **j**   **setlinejoin**
Sets the line join parameter in the graphics state. *linejoin* is an integer and has a default value of 0.

linecap **J**   **setlinecap**
Sets the line cap parameter in the graphics state. *linecap* is an integer and has a default value of 0.

miterlimit **M**   **setmiterlimit**
Sets the miter limit parameter in the graphics state. *miterlimit* is a number that must be greater than or equal to 1, and has a default value of 10.

linewidth **w**   **setlinewidth**
Sets the line width parameter in the graphics state. *linewidth* is a number and has a default value of 1.

7.4 Color operators

Colors may be specified in any of three color spaces: grayscale, red–green–blue (RGB), or cyan–magenta–yellow–black (CMYK). The default fill and stroke colors are both black.

Color operators may appear between path objects and inside text objects. They may not appear within path objects.

gray **g** **setgray** (fill)
Sets the gray tint to use for filling paths. *gray* is a number between 0 (black) and 1 (white).

gray **G** **setgray** (stroke)
Sets the gray tint to use for stroking paths. *gray* is a number between 0 (black) and 1 (white).

cyan magenta yellow black **k** **setcmykcolor** (fill)
Sets the color to use for filling paths. Each operand must be a number between 0 (minimum intensity) and 1 (maximum intensity).

cyan magenta yellow black **K** **setcmykcolor** (stroke)
Sets the color to use for stroking paths. Each operand must be a number between 0 (minimum intensity) and 1 (maximum intensity).

red green blue **rg** **setrgbcolor** (fill)
Sets the color to use for filling paths. Each operand must be a number between 0 (minimum intensity) and 1 (maximum intensity).

red green blue **RG** **setrgbcolor** (stroke)
Sets the color to use for stroking paths. Each operand must be a number between 0 (minimum intensity) and 1 (maximum intensity).

7.5 Path operators

Paths are used to represent lines, curves, and regions. A path consists of a series of path segment operators describing where marks will appear on the page, followed by a path painting operator, which actually marks the path in one of several ways. A path may be composed of one or more disconnected sections, referred to as *subpaths*. An example of a path with two subpaths is a path containing two parallel line segments.

Path segments may be straight lines or curves. Curves in PDF files are represented as cubic Bézier curves. A cubic Bézier curve is specified by the *x*- and *y*-coordinates of four points: the two endpoints of the curve (the current point and P_3) and two *control points* (points P_1 and P_2), as shown in Figure 7.6.

Figure 7.6 *Bézier curve*

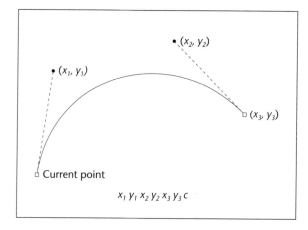

Once these four points are specified, the cubic Bézier curve *R*(t) is generated by varying the parameter *t* from 0 to 1 in the following equation:

$$R(t) \; = \; (1-t)^3 \, P_0 + 3t \, (1-t)^2 \, P_1 + 3t^2 (1-t) \, P_2 + t^3 P_3$$

In this equation, P_0 is the current point before the curve is drawn. When the parameter *t* has the value 0, *R*(t) = P_0 (the current point). When *t*=1, *R*(t)=P_3. The curve does not, in general, pass through the two control points P_1 and P_2.

Bézier curves have two desirable properties. First, the curve is contained within the convex hull of the control points. The convex hull is most easily visualized as the polygon obtained by stretching a rubber band around the outside of the four points defining the curve. This property allows rapid testing of whether the curve is completely outside the visible region, and so does not have to be rendered. Second, Bézier curves can be very quickly split into smaller pieces for rapid rendering.

Note   *In the remainder of this book, the term* Bézier curve *means cubic Bézier curve.*

Paths are subject to and may also be used for clipping. Path clipping operators replace the current clipping path with the intersection of the current clipping path and the current path.

<path> ::=   <subpath>+
                {path clipping operator}
                <path painting operator>

<subpath> ::=   m <path segment operator except m and re>* |
                re

7.5.1 Path segment operators

All operands are numbers that are coordinates in user space.

$x\ y$ **m** **moveto**
Moves the current point to (x, y), omitting any connecting line segment.

$x\ y$ **l** (operator is lowercase L) **lineto**
Appends a straight line segment from the current point to (x, y). The new current point is (x, y).

$x_1\ y_1\ x_2\ y_2\ x_3\ y_3$ **c** **curveto**
Appends a Bézier curve to the path. The curve extends from the current point to (x_3, y_3) using (x_1, y_1) and (x_2, y_2) as the Bézier control points, as shown in Figure 7.6. The new current point is (x_3, y_3).

$x_2\ y_2\ x_3\ y_3$ **v** **curveto** (first control point coincides with initial point on curve)
Appends a Bézier curve to the current path between the current point and the point (x_3, y_3) using the current point and (x_2, y_2) as the Bézier control points, as shown in Figure 7.7. The new current point is (x_3, y_3).

Figure 7.7 v *operator*

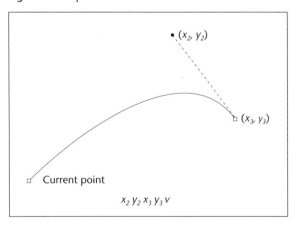

$x_1\ y_1\ x_3\ y_3$ **y** **curveto** (second control point coincides with final point on curve)
Appends a Bézier curve to the current path between the current point
and the point (x_3, y_3) using (x_1, y_1) and (x_3, y_3) as the Bézier control
points, as shown in Figure 7.8. The new current point is (x_3, y_3).

Figure 7.8 y *operator*

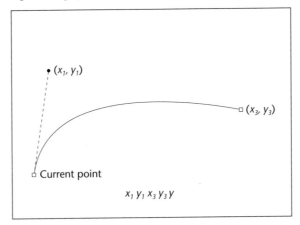

$x\ y\ width\ height$ **re** Adds the rectangle to the current path. *width* and *height* are distances in
user space.

— **h** **closepath**
Closes the current subpath by appending a straight line segment from
the current point to the starting point of the subpath.

7.5.2 Path painting operators

Paths may be stroked and/or filled. As in the PostScript language,
painting completely obscures any marks already on the page under the
region that is painted.

Stroking draws a line along the path, using the line width, dash pattern,
miter limit, line cap style, line join style, and stroke color from the
graphics state. The line drawn when a path is stroked is centered on the
path. If a path consists of multiple subpaths, each is treated separately.

The process of filling a path paints the entire region enclosed by the path, using the fill color. If a path consists of several disconnected subpaths, each is filled separately. Any open subpaths are implicitly closed before being filled. Closing is accomplished by adding a segment between the first and last points on the path. For a simple path, it is clear what lies inside the path and should be painted by a fill. For more complicated paths, it is not so obvious. One of two rules is used to determine which points lie inside a path.

The *non-zero winding number rule* uses the following test to determine whether a given point is inside a path and should be painted. Conceptually, a ray is drawn in any direction from the point in question to infinity and the points where the ray crosses path segments are examined. Starting from a count of zero, add one to the count each time a path segment crosses the ray from left to right, and subtract one from the count each time a path segment crosses the ray from right to left. If the ray encounters a path segment that coincides with it, the result is undefined. In this case, a ray in another direction can be picked, since all rays are equivalent. After counting all the crossings, if the result is zero then the point is outside the path. The effect of using this rule on various paths is illustrated in Figure 7.9. The non-zero winding number rule is used by the PostScript language **fill** operator.

Figure 7.9 *Non-zero winding number rule*

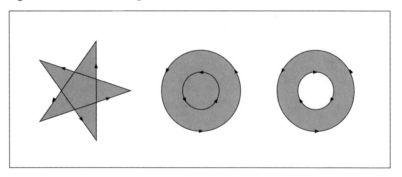

The *even–odd rule* uses a slightly different strategy. The same calculation is made as for the non-zero winding number rule, but instead of testing for a result of zero, a test is made as to whether the result is even or odd. If the result is odd, the point is inside the path; if the result is even, the point is outside. The result of applying this rule to various paths is illustrated in Figure 7.10. The even–odd rule is used by the PostScript language **eofill** operator.

Figure 7.10 *Even–odd rule*

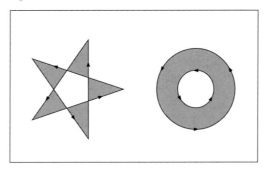

— **n** Ends the path without filling or stroking it.

— **S** **stroke**
Strokes the path.

— **s** **closepath** and **stroke**
Similar to the **S** operator, but closes the path before stroking it.

— **f** **fill**
Fills the path, using the non-zero winding number rule to determine the region to fill.

— **f*** **eofill**
Fills the path, using the even–odd rule to determine the region to fill.

— **B** **fill** and **stroke**

— **b** **closepath**, **fill**, and **stroke**

— **B*** **eofill** and **stroke**

— **b*** **closepath**, **eofill**, and **stroke**

7.5.3 Path clipping operators

Path clipping operators cause the current clipping path to be replaced with the intersection of the current clipping path and the path. A path is made into a clipping path by inserting a path clipping operator between the last path segment operator and the path painting operator.

Although the path clipping operator appears before the path painting operator, the path clipping operator does not alter the clipping path at the point it appears. Rather, it modifies the effect of the path painting operator. After the path is filled or stroked by the path painting operator, it is set to be the current clipping path. If the path is both filled and stroked, the painting is done in that order before making the path the current clipping path.

The definition of the clipping path and all subsequent operations it is to affect should be contained between a pair of **q** and **Q** operators. Execution of the **Q** operator causes the clipping path to revert to that saved by the **q** operator, before the clipping path was modified.

— **W   clip**
Uses the non-zero winding number rule to determine which regions are inside the clipping path.

— **W*   eoclip**
Uses the even–odd rule to determine which regions are inside the clipping path.

7.6   Text state

The text state is composed of those graphics state parameters that affect only text. See Section 7.2, "Graphics state" for further information on the graphics state. Each of the items in the text state is described in the following sections.

7.6.1 Character spacing

Character spacing modifies the spacing between characters in a string, by adding or removing a specified amount of space between each pair of characters. Character spacing is a number specified in text space units. Figure 7.11 shows the effect of character spacing.

Figure 7.11 *Character spacing*

Character	0 (default)
Character	5

7.6.2 Horizontal scaling

Horizontal scaling adjusts the width of characters, by stretching or shrinking them in the horizontal direction. The scaling is specified as a percent of the normal width of the characters, with 100 being the normal width. Figure 7.12 shows the effect of horizontal scaling.

Figure 7.12 *Horizontal scaling*

Word	100 (default)
WordWord	50

7.6.3 Leading

Leading specifies the vertical distance between the baselines of adjacent lines of text, as shown in Figure 7.13. Leading is measured in text space units.

Figure 7.13 *Leading*

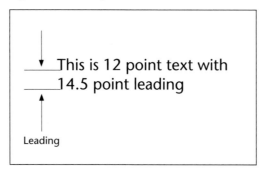

7.6.4 Text font

Specifies the font used to draw text.

7.6.5 Text matrix

The text matrix specifies the transformation from text space to user space. See Section 3.3, "Text space."

7.6.6 Text rendering mode

Determines whether text is stroked, filled, or used as a clipping path.

Note *The rendering mode has no effect on text displayed using a Type 3 font.*

The rendering modes are shown in Figure 7.14. In the figure, a stroke color of black and a fill color of light gray are used. After one of the clipping modes is used for text rendering, the text object must be ended using the **ET** operator before changing the text rendering mode.

Note *For the clipping modes (4–7), a series of lines has been drawn through the characters in Figure 7.14 to show where the clipping occurs.*

Figure 7.14 *Text rendering modes*

	Rendering mode	Description
R	0	Fill text
R	1	Stroke text
R	2	Fill and stroke text
	3	Text with no fill and no stroke (invisible)
R	4	Fill text and add it to the clipping path
R	5	Stroke text and add it to the clipping path
R	6	Fill and stroke text and add it to the clipping path
	7	Add text to the clipping path

7.6.7 Text rise

Text rise specifies the amount, in text space units, to move the baseline up or down from its default location. Positive values of text rise move the baseline up. Adjustments to the baseline are useful for drawing superscripts or subscripts. The default location of the baseline can be restored by setting the text rise to 0. Figure 7.15 illustrates the effect of the text rise, which is set using the **Ts** operator.

Figure 7.15 *Text rise*

This text is ^{superscripted}	(This text is) Tj 5 Ts (superscripted) Tj
This text is _{subscripted}	(This text is) Tj –5 Ts (subscripted) Tj
This text moves around	(This) Tj –5 Ts (text) Tj 5 Ts (moves) Tj 0 Ts (around) Tj

7.6.8 Text size

Specifies the character size, in text space units, when text is drawn.

7.6.9 Word spacing

Modifies the spacing between words in a string, by adding or removing space from each ASCII space character (character code 32) in the string. Word spacing is a number specified in text space units. Figure 7.16 illustrates the effect of word spacing.

Figure 7.16 *Effect of word spacing*

Word Space	0 (default)
Word Space	10

7.7 Text operators

A PDF text object consists of operators that specify character strings, movement of the current point, and text state. A text object begins with the **BT** operator and ends with the **ET** operator.

```
<text object> ::=   BT
                    <text operator or graphics state operator>*
                    ET
```

Note *The graphics state operators* **q**, **Q***, and* **cm** *cannot appear within a text object.*

When **BT** is encountered, the text matrix is initialized to the identity matrix. When **ET** is encountered, the text matrix is discarded. Text objects cannot be nested—a second **BT** cannot appear before an **ET**.

Note *If a page does not contain any text, no text operators (including operators that merely set the text state) may be present in the page description.*

7.7.1 Text object operators

— **BT** Begins a text object. Initializes the text matrix to the identity matrix.

— **ET** Ends a text object. Discards the text matrix.

7.7.2 Text state operators

These operators set the text-specific parameters in the graphics state.

Note *These operators can appear outside of text objects, and the values they set are retained across text objects on a single page. Like other graphics state parameters, the values are initialized to the default values at the beginning of each page.*

charSpace **Tc** Set character spacing
Sets the character spacing parameter in the graphics state. Character spacing is used, together with word spacing, by the **Tj**, **TJ**, and ' operators to calculate spacing of text within a line. *charSpace* is a number expressed in text space units and has a default value of 0.

fontname size **Tf** Set font and size

Sets the text font and text size in the graphics state. There is no default value for either *fontname* or *size*; they must be selected using **Tf** before drawing any text. *fontname* is a resource name. *size* is a number expressed in text space units.

leading **TL** Set text leading

Sets the leading parameter in the graphics state. Leading is used by the **T***, ', and " operators to calculate the position of the next line of text. The **TL** operator need not be used in a PDF file unless the **T***, ', or " operators are used. *leading* is a number expressed in text space units and has a default value of 0.

render **Tr** Set the text rendering mode

render is an integer and has a default value of 0.

rise **Ts** Set text rise

Moves the baseline vertically by *rise* units. This operator is used for superscripting and subscripting. *rise* is a number expressed in text space units and has a default value of 0.

wordSpace **Tw** Set word spacing

Sets the word spacing parameter in the graphics state. Word spacing is used, together with character spacing, by the **Tj**, **TJ**, and ' operators to calculate spacing of text within a line. *wordSpace* is a number expressed in text space units and has a default value of 0.

scale **Tz** Set horizontal scaling

Sets the horizontal scaling parameter in the graphics state. *scale* is a number expressed in percent of the normal scaling and has a default value of 100.

7.7.3   Text positioning operators

A text object keeps track of the current point and the start of the current line. The text string operators move the current point like the various forms of the PostScript language **show** operator. Operators that move the start of the current line move the current point as well.

Note   *These operators may appear only within text objects.*

t_x t_y **Td** Moves to the start of the next line, offset from the start of the current line by (t_x, t_y). t_x and t_y are numbers expressed in text space units.

$t_x\ t_y$ **TD** Moves to the start of the next line, offset from the start of the current line by (t_x, t_y). As a side effect, this sets the leading parameter in the graphics state, used by the **T***, ', and " operators. t_x and t_y are numbers expressed in text space units. The value assigned to the leading is the negative of t_y.

$a\ b\ c\ d\ e\ f$ **Tm** Sets the text matrix and sets the current point and line start position to the origin. The operands are all numbers, and the default matrix is [1 0 0 1 0 0]. Although the operands specify a matrix, they are passed as six numbers, not an array.

Note *The matrix specified by the operands passed to the **Tm** operator is not concatenated onto the current text matrix, but replaces it.*

— **T*** Moves to the start of the next line. The *x*-coordinate is the same as that of the most recent **TD**, **Td**, or **Tm** operation, and the *y*-coordinate equals that of the current line minus the leading.

7.7.4   Text string operators

These operators draw text on the page. Although it is possible to pass individual characters to the text string operators, text searching performs significantly better if the text is grouped by word and paragraph.

PDF supports the same conventions as the PostScript language for specifying non-printable ASCII characters. That is, a character can be represented by an escape sequence, as enumerated in Table 4.1 on page 26.

Note *If a current point has not been established in a text object (using the **Tm**, **Td**, or **TD** operators) before text is drawn in that object, the text will be displayed at the page origin.*

string **Tj** Shows text string, using the character and word spacing parameters from the graphics state.

string ' Moves to next line and shows text string, using the character and word spacing parameters from the graphics state.

$a_w\ a_c$ *string* " Moves to next line and shows text string. a_w and a_c are numbers expressed in text space units. a_w specifies the additional space width and a_c specifies the additional space between characters, otherwise specified using the **Tw** and **Tc** operators.

Note   *The values specified by a_w and a_c remain the word and character spacings after the " operator is executed, as though they were set using the **Tc** and **Tw** operators.*

[number or string ...] **TJ**   Shows text string, allowing individual character positioning, and using the character and word spacing parameters from the graphics state. For each element of the array that is passed as an operand, if the element is a string, shows the string. If it is a number, moves the current point to the *left* by the given amount, expressed in thousandths of an em. (An *em* is a typographic unit of measurement equal to the size of a font—for example, in a 12-point font an em is 12 points.)

Each character is first justified according to any character and word spacing settings made with the **Tc** or **Tw** operators, and then any numeric offset present in the array passed to the **TJ** operator is applied. An example of the use of **TJ** is shown in Figure 7.17.

Note   *When using the* **TJ** *operator, the x-coordinate of the current point after drawing a character and moving by any specified offset must not be less than the x-coordinate of the current point before the character was drawn.*

Figure 7.17 *Operation of* **TJ** *operator*

AWAY again	[(AWAY again)] TJ
AWAY again	[(A) 120 (W) 120 (A) 95 (Y again)] TJ

7.8   XObject operator

The **Do** operator permits the execution of an arbitrary object whose data is encapsulated within a PDF object. The currently supported XObjects are images and PostScript language forms, discussed in Section 6.8.6, "XObject resources."

xobject **Do**   Executes the specified XObject. *xobject* must be a resource name.

7.9   In-line image operators

In addition to the image resource described in 6.8.6, "XObject resources," PDF supports in-line images. An in-line image consists of the operator **BI**, followed by image resource key–value pairs, followed by the operator **ID**, followed by the image data, followed by **EI**:

```
<in-line image> ::=  BI
                     <image resource key–value pairs>
                     ID
                     {<lines of data>}+
                     EI
```

Note   *If an in-line image does not use ASCIIHexDecode or ASCII85Decode as one of its filters,* **ID** *should be followed by a single space. The character following the space is interpreted as the first byte of image data.*

Image data may be encoded using any of the standard PDF filters. The key–value pairs provided in an in-line image should not include keys specific to resources: **Type**, **Subtype**, and **Name**. Within in-line images, the standard key names may be replaced by the shorter names listed in Table 7.3. These short names may not be used in image resources, however.

Note   *For in-line images with indexed color spaces, the color table must be specified using a hexadecimal string.*

Table 7.3 *Abbreviations for in-line image names*

Name	Abbreviated name
ASCIIHexDecode	**AHx**
ASCII85Decode	**A85**
BitsPerComponent	**BPC**
CCITTFaxDecode	**CCF**
ColorSpace	**CS**
DCTDecode	**DCT**
Decode	**D**
DecodeParms	**DP**
DeviceCMYK	**CMYK**
DeviceGray	**G**

DeviceRGB	RGB
Filter	F
Height	H
ImageMask	IM
Indexed	I
Interpolate	I
LZWDecode	LZW
RunLengthDecode	RL
Width	W

Note   *The in-line format should be used only for small images (4K or less) because viewer applications have less flexibility when managing in-line image data.*

In-line images, like image resources, are one unit wide and one unit high in user space and drawn at the origin. Images are sized and positioned by transforming user space using the **cm** operator.

— **BI** Begins image

— **ID** Begins image data

— **EI** Ends image

Example 7.1 shows a 17×17 sample in-line image. The image is an 8-bit per component RGB image that has been LZW and ASCII85 encoded. The **cm** operator has been used to scale the image to render at a size of 17×17 user space units and located at an *x*-coordinate of 298 and a *y*-coordinate of 388. The **q** and **Q** operators limit the scope of the **cm** operator's effect to resizing the image.

Example 7.1 *In-line image*

```
q
17 0 0 17 298 388 cm
BI
/W 17
/H 17
/BPC 8
/CS /RGB
/F [/A85 /LZW]
ID
J1/gKA>.]AN&J?]-<HW]aRVcg*bb.\eKAdVV%/PcZ/+o:4MDHkB<kM0*0[niJ-f2\
```

```
<gl38;.c/h"LdncP[8">Mop)258E%21?6ak773GKLiXNc%Uc%L*cW!b7,[^'b>DoM
&bsN,4Vh<nU1;F68pMH!D^35cnkXP&b)\@[@HN1n4HML4)-u?KGp2./Vl[8@]k?`;k
ec#P;JlVg%YQ3q:#p@<AOq)E25H]44Bh.@,N1rJIO`"pmkgHOlCUDV6qC`oD$hU*
+,H_fC,F:/CRbWJ,C&J4D]_):,U\GqM"*Ngm=^ggkaOccTo75bTuH5k7Qj&9E5.>a
%mpQ>a5Q8Fb*=fH)Wp#MW89a]rS<51"17&3S\qCfG7Oahg-,l,=Um5.`3AHMPf.;$
#a"!!bjtl]-or.TJhWWLOomt2B+:R9^,?5YptQs]"(7"&%3g(b1lCELhD#kBaP:8;
6i!NUO[h)`6Ng1%0akXT5W079iM`&"%g([h;N'OS<\+TS!1GVS!Z9WLLP)hL*tKRb
N'<2paTam=jAAYZOMKq:,WrA(%Le$O!*gHR,"Q`8M;`^K+\@6(-pe%*a?)flA2$%S&
>9qi71%G>/FkpL5VNJW1uLA?!TZA(9N74X9G!<%o4@lJCQMMeCB6::kK9D1Klo
W*E,sjZtM9)OFZOO6%cLo2bjH57?L;l(%<qcKZ!j](_=H%=?m$u3<U"O,S5f8OMJhc
%YS?m64o;&%EE(B^sGV;KL*El)$n-YlOkq[Gec-CipbWMNZuj,4,rpP93PJB%Ll>>
KFgO"N^>_X1(3-@\hfBKkh%tU,A?j-Nhe)e5_>*"AQ$g>5\NB9_[tTRNrp6K4q'f'
qjNTk+RDFS6g5`4]YM>n%V26hMir]R4=a_B"<^et%q9eQ3/rS<2F<B*\I(5*,Y6oZ
BB2oJ6B^<t*Z^'tBS7aq69pu.Lr*R3,7.mGLaNc933kpZ"EpG&O[c<8rr%9-9i)1
R.s(4KE3&d&7hb*7[%Ct2HCqC~>
EI
Q
```

7.10   Type 3 font operators

Type 3 font operators can only be used within the character definitions
inside a Type 3 font resource. Each Type 3 font definition must begin
with either a **d0** or **d1** operator. See Section 5.7 of the *PostScript Language
Reference Manual, Second Edition* for details.

w_x w_y **d0**   (d zero) **setcharwidth**
The operands are both numbers.

w_x w_y ll_x ll_y ur_x ur_y **d1**   (d one) **setcachedevice**
The operands are all numbers.

Section II

Optimizing PDF Files

CHAPTER **8**

General Techniques for Optimizing PDF Files

The first section of this book describes the syntax allowed in a PDF file. In many cases there is more than one way to represent a particular construct, and the previous chapters do not indicate which alternative is preferred. This section describes techniques to optimize PDF files. Most optimizations reduce the size of a PDF file, reduce the amount of memory needed to display pages, or improve the speed with which pages are drawn. Some optimizations, such as sharing of resources, allow a viewer application to display a document when it may not have otherwise been possible in low memory situations. A few optimizations improve the appearance of pages.

This chapter contains techniques that can be generally applied to PDF files. Following chapters discuss optimizations specifically for text, graphics, and images.

While it may not be possible to take advantage of all the techniques described here, it is worth taking more time producing a PDF file to improve its viewing performance. A PDF file will be produced only once but may be viewed many times.

File size is a good gauge of the level of optimization, but of course the most accurate measure is the time it takes to view and print the pages of a document.

8.1 Use short names

Names in PDF files specify resources, including fonts, forms, and images. Whenever a name is used, it should contain as few characters as possible. This minimizes the space needed to store references to the object.

Instead of specifying a name as:

```
/FirstFontInPage4
/SecondImageInPage8
```

use names such as:

```
/F1
/Im8
```

Resource names need not be unique throughout a document. The names of resource objects must be unique within a given resource type within a single page. For example, the names of all fonts on a page must be unique.

8.2 Use direct and indirect objects appropriately

As mentioned in Chapter 4, objects contained in composite objects such as arrays and dictionaries can either be specified directly in the composite object or referred to indirectly. Using indirect objects frequently improves performance and reduces the size of a PDF file. In addition, programs that produce PDF files sometimes must write an object into a PDF file before the object's value is known. Indirect objects are useful in this situation.

8.2.1 Minimizing object size

Although PDF allows random access to objects in a file, it does not permit random access to the substructure that may be present in a single object, such as the individual key–value pairs in a dictionary object. If a PDF viewer application needs to access a particular piece of information contained in an object, it reads the entire object. However, if it encounters an indirect object reference, it will not read the indirect object until needed. Using indirect objects minimizes the amount of extra data a PDF viewer application must read before locating the desired information.

As an example, if a PDF viewer application needs to obtain the PostScript language name of a font, it must search the appropriate Font dictionary object. If (in that dictionary object) the **Widths** array is specified directly, the application must read the entire array. If the **Widths** array is specified by an indirect reference, the application only needs to read the few bytes that specify the indirect reference and can avoid reading the **Widths** array itself.

In general, using indirect references improves the performance of a PDF file. However, there is some overhead associated with locating an indirect object, and an indirect object takes up more space than a direct object in a PDF file. Because of this, small objects should not be specified indirectly. A rough rule of thumb is that arrays with more than five elements and dictionaries with more than three key–value pairs should be stored as indirect objects.

8.2.2   Sharing objects

Indirect objects can be referred to from more than one location in a file. Because of this, using indirect objects can decrease the size of a PDF file by defining an object only once and making multiple references to it.

As an example, suppose each page in a document require the same ProcSets. Each page's Resources dictionary can refer to the same ProcSet array indirectly instead of duplicating the array.

8.2.3   Placeholder for an unknown value

Indirect objects can also be used when an object must be written at one location in a file, but its value will not be known until later in the process of writing the file. The best example of this situation is the **Length** key in the dictionary of a Stream object. The dictionary must be placed in the file ahead of the stream data itself, and must include the **Length** key, which specifies the length of the stream that follows. It may not be possible to know the length of the stream until after the data has been written, however. By specifying the value of the **Length** key as an indirect object, the length of the stream can be written after the stream.

8.3   Take advantage of combined operators

PDF provides several operators that combine the function of two or more other operators. For example, PDF defines operators that close (**h**) and stroke (**S**) a path, but also provides an operator that performs both operations (**s**). These combined operators should be used whenever possible. Table 8.1 lists the combined operators provided by PDF. Some operators in the table require one or more operands; the operands have been omitted from the table.

Table 8.1 *Optimized operator combinations*

Use...	Instead of...
s	h S
b	h B
TD	Td TL
TJ	Repeated series of **Tj** and **Td** operators
'	**Td Tj** or **T* Tj**
"	**Tc Tw Td Tj**

Note   *To both fill and stroke a path, the combination operators must be used. Using the fill operator followed by the stroke operator does not work. The fill operator ends the path, leaving nothing for the stroke operator to stroke. Unlike the PostScript language, PDF does not allow you to save the path, fill it, restore the path, and stroke it, because the current path is not part of the PDF graphics state.*

8.4   Remove unnecessary clipping paths

Whenever anything is drawn on a page, all marks are made inside the current clipping path. When a clipping path other than the default (the crop box) is specified, rendering speed is reduced. If a portion of a page requires the use of a clipping path other than the default, the default clipping path should be restored as soon as possible. Text, graphics, and images are all clipped to the current clipping path, so it is important for the performance of all three to not use unnecessary clipping paths.

Restoration of a clipping path can be accomplished by saving the graphics state (including the clipping path) using the **q** operator before setting the new clipping path, and subsequently using the **Q** operator to restore the previous clipping path as soon as the new clipping path is no longer needed.

Note   *Remember that the **Q** operator restores more than just the clipping path. See Section 7.2, "Graphics state" for a list of the graphics state parameters restored by the **Q** operator.*

8.5   Omit unnecessary spaces

Spaces are unnecessary before (, after), and before and after [and]. This slightly reduces the size of files.

8.6 Omit default values

A number of the parameters that affect drawing have default values that are initialized at the start of every page. (See Sections 7.3, "Graphics state operators," 7.4, "Color operators," and 7.7.2, "Text state operators.") For example, the default stroke and fill colors are both black. When drawing, do not explicitly set a drawing parameter unless the default value is not the desired value.

Similarly, many PDF objects are represented by dictionaries and some of the keys in these dictionaries have default values. Omit any keys whose default value is the desired value.

Omitting unnecessary key–value pairs and graphics and text state operators reduces the size of a PDF file and the time needed to process it.

8.7 Take advantage of forms

PDF files may contain forms, which are arbitrary collections of PDF operators that draw text, graphics, or images. The structure of a Form object is discussed in Section 6.8.6, "XObject resources." A Form object may be used to draw the same marks in one or more locations on one or more pages.

Forms can be used, for example, to draw a logo, a heading for stationery, or a traditional form. The location and appearance of a form is controlled by the CTM in effect when the form is drawn.

The use of forms can reduce the size of a PDF file. In addition, forms that contain an XUID can be cached by PDF viewer applications and PostScript printers, improving rendering speed if the form is used multiple times.

8.8 Limit the precision of real numbers

The pixel size on most monitors is 1/72 of an inch, or 1 unit in default user space. The dot size on printers and imagesetters generally ranges from 1/300 of an inch (.24 units) to 1/2400 of an inch (.03 units). For this range of devices, it suffices to store coordinates to two digits to the right of the decimal point. However, because coordinates can be scaled, they should be written using more than two digits, but generally not more than five. Acrobat Exchange and Acrobat Reader store numbers in a fixed format that allows 16 bits for a fraction, which is equivalent to four or five decimal places.

Most monitors and printers cannot produce more than 256 shades of a given color component. Color component values should not be written using more than four decimal places.

8.9 Write parameters only when they change

Graphics state operators should be written only when the corresponding graphics state parameters change. Changes to graphics state parameters typically occur both when the application explicitly changes them and when the graphics state is restored using the **Q** operator.

When explicit changes are made to the value of a graphics state parameter, new and old values of the parameter should be compared with the precision with which they will be written, not their internal precision.

A pair of **q** and **Q** operators is commonly used to bracket a sequence of operators that uses a non-default clipping path. The **q** operator saves the default clipping path, and the **Q** operator discards the clipping path when it is no longer needed. However, the **q** and **Q** operators save and restore the entire graphics state, not just the clipping path. To avoid unnecessarily setting all graphics state parameters to achieve a known state after a **Q** operator, an application that produces PDF files may wish to maintain its own graphics state stack mimicking the PDF graphics state stack. This enables the application to determine the values of all graphics state parameters at all times, and only write operators to change graphics state parameters that do not have the desired value after the **Q** operator.

8.10 Don't draw outside the crop box

Objects entirely outside the crop box do not appear on screen or on the final printout. Nevertheless, if such objects are present in a PDF file, each time the page is drawn, time is spent determining if any portion of them is visible. Simply omit any objects that are entirely outside of the crop box, instead of relying on clipping to keep them from being drawn.

8.11   Consider target device resolution

When producing a PDF file, it is extremely important to consider the device that is the primary target of the document contained in the file. A number of decisions may be made differently depending on whether the document will be primarily viewed on a low-resolution device such as a computer screen or printed to an extremely high-resolution device such as an imagesetter.

If the primary target of the document is a computer screen, users are generally most interested in small file sizes and fast display, and are willing to accept somewhat reduced resolution in exchange for those. If, on the other hand, the primary target is a 1200-dpi imagesetter, file size and drawing time are not as important as obtaining the highest quality possible.

PDF, like the PostScript language, allows graphics objects to be drawn at an arbitrary size and scaled to the desired size. It is often convenient to design objects at a standard size and scale them for a particular situation. Greatly reducing the size of an object, however, can result in unnecessary detail and slow drawing. Choose a level of detail that is appropriate for both monitors and common printer resolutions. In some cases it may be appropriate to replace a complex element of a page with an equivalent image.

Decisions related to the target device primarily affect text, images, and blends. They are discussed further in the following chapters.

8.12   Share resources

Typically, many pages of a document share the same set of fonts. A PDF file will be smaller, display faster, and use less memory if the page's Resources dictionaries refer to the same Font objects. Similarly, if multiple fonts use the same custom encoding, one Encoding object should be shared. The same holds true for ProcSets—if multiple pages require the same combination of ProcSets, they should refer to the same ProcSet array.

8.13   Store common Page attributes in the Pages object

Several Page attributes need not be specified directly in the Page object, but can be inherited from a parent Pages object. Attributes that are the same for all pages in a document may be written once in the root Pages object. If a particular page has a different value, it can directly specify that value and override its parent's value. For example, all pages except one in a document might have the same media box. This value can be stored in the root Pages object, and the media box for the odd-size page can be specified directly in its Page object.

CHAPTER **9**

Optimizing Text

Most text optimizations relate to using appropriate operators and taking advantage of the automatic line, character, and word spacing operators supported by PDF. A few optimizations relate to searching.

9.1 Don't produce unnecessary text objects

A PDF viewer application initializes the text environment at the beginning of each text object, and this initialization takes some time. Minimizing the number of text objects used reduces this overhead and reduces file size.

It is not necessary to end one text object and begin another whenever the text matrix is changed using the **Tm** operator. Instead, the text matrix can be changed inside the text object. For example, to create a text object containing several lines of text at various rotations, the following text object could be used:

Example 9.1 *Changing the text matrix inside a text object*

```
BT
/F13 24 Tf
200 100 Td
(Horizontal text) Tj
0.866 0.5 -0.5 0.866 186 150 Tm
(Text rotated 30 degrees counterclockwise) Tj
0.5 0.866 -0.866 0.5 150 186 Tm
(Text rotated 60 degrees counterclockwise) Tj
0 1 -1 0 100 200 Tm
(Text rotated 90 degrees counterclockwise) Tj
ET
```

This sequence draws the text in whatever font has the name F13, at a size of 24 points. Keep in mind that the matrix specified using the **Tm** operator replaces the text matrix; it is not concatenated onto the text matrix.

Similarly, font and most other graphics state parameters can change inside a text object. There is one exception—if one of the clipping text rendering modes is used, the text object must end before changing the text rendering mode again.

9.2 Use automatic leading

Several of the text string operators make use of the text leading setting to position the drawing point at the start of the next line of text. This makes generating multiple lines of text easy and compact. Use automatic leading whenever possible. The ' and " operators automatically move to the next line of text, as defined by the leading, and the **T*** operator can be used to manually move to the next line of text. Define leading using either the **TD** or **TL** operators.

Note   *Don't use the **TD** or **TL** operator unless you use a text operator that has automatic leading.*

For example, the text object in Example 9.2 can be more efficiently written using automatic leading and the ' operator as in Example 9.3.

Example 9.2 *Multiple lines of text without automatic leading*

```
BT
/F13 12 Tf
200 400 Td
(First line of text) Tj
0 -14 Td
(Second line of text) Tj
0 -14 Td
(Third line of text) Tj
0 -14 Td
(Fourth line of text) Tj
ET
```

Example 9.3 *Multiple lines of text using automatic leading*

```
BT
/F13 12 Tf
200 414 Td
14 TL
(First line of text) '
(Second line of text) '
(Third line of text) '
(Fourth line of text) '
ET
```

Note in Example 9.3 that the initial point has been offset vertically by one line. This is because the ' operator moves to the next line before drawing the text.

If it is not possible to use either the ' or " operators to draw a line of text (for example, because the **TJ** operator is used to adjust spacing between particular characters within the line), you can still use the **T*** operator, which advances the point to the beginning of the next line, using the current leading. For example, the text object in Example 9.4 can be more efficiently written using automatic leading and the **T*** operator, as in Example 9.5.

Example 9.4 TJ *operator without automatic leading*

```
BT
/F13 12 Tf
200 700 Td
[(First line) 100 ( of text)] TJ
0 -14 Td
[(Second line) 50 ( of text)] TJ
0 -14 Td
[(Third line) 40 ( of text)] TJ
0 -14 Td
[(Fourth line) 50 ( of text)] TJ
ET
```

Example 9.5 *Use of the* **T*** *operator*

```
BT
/F13 12 Tf
200 700 Td
14 TL
[(First line) 100 ( of text)] TJ
T*
[(Second line) 50 ( of text)] TJ
T*
[(Third line) 40 ( of text)] TJ
T*
[(Fourth line) 50 ( of text)] TJ
ET
```

Finally, you can set the leading in either of two ways. The **TL** operator sets the leading directly, while the **TD** operator sets the leading as a side effect of moving the line start position. The methods shown in Example 9.6 and Example 9.7 are equivalent.

Example 9.6 *Using the* **TL** *operator to set leading*

```
BT
/F13 12 Tf
200 500 Td
14 TL
[(First line) 100 ( of text)] TJ
T*
[(Second line) 50 ( of text)] TJ
T*
[(Third line) 40 ( of text)] TJ
T*
[(Fourth line) 50 ( of text)] TJ
ET
```

Example 9.7 *Using the* **TD** *operator to set leading*

```
BT
/F13 12 Tf
200 500 Td
[(First line) 100 ( of text)] TJ
0 -14 TD
[(Second line) 50 ( of text)] TJ
T*
[(Third line) 40 ( of text)] TJ
T*
[(Fourth line) 50 ( of text)] TJ
ET
```

When using the **TD** operator to set the leading, keep in mind that any horizontal component supplied as an operand to **TD** affects the movement of the drawing point, but not the leading. As a result, the commands **0 –14 TD** and **10 –14 TD** both set the leading to 14, although in the latter case the drawing point is ten units to the right of where it is in the former case.

9.3   Take advantage of text spacing operators

The **Tc** and **Tw** operators adjust the spacing between characters and the spacing between words, respectively. Use these operators to make constant adjustments on one or more lines of text. Example 9.8 shows a text object in which one half unit of space has been added between characters on a line and two units between words.

Example 9.8 *Character and word spacing using the* **Tc** *and* **Tw** *operators*

```
BT
/F13 12 Tf
200 514 Td
14 TL
.5 Tc
2 Tw
(Line of text) '
(Line of text) '
ET
```

Equivalently, the same two lines of text could be produced using the " operator instead of the **Tc**, **Tw**, and ' operators, as shown in Example 9.9.

Example 9.9 *Character and word spacing using the* " *operator*

```
BT
/F13 12 Tf
200 514 Td
14 TL
2   .5 (Line of text) "
(Line of text) '
ET
```

Using the " operator is preferable if entire lines of text are being written, because it is more compact. If more than one text string operator is used to produce a line of text, the " operator can be used to position the first string of the line and **Tj** or **TJ** for subsequent strings. Remember that the " operator changes the character and word spacing settings for subsequent **Tj**, **TJ**, and ' operators.

9.4 Don't replace spaces between words

When deciding how to represent a line of text in a PDF file, keep in mind that text can be searched. In order to search text accurately, breaks between words must be found. For this reason, it is best to leave spaces in strings, instead of replacing them with an operator that moves the drawing point.

For example, text containing three words could be drawn by:

    (A few words) Tj

Or, replacing the spaces between words with movements of the drawing point:

    [(A) -300 (few) -300 (words)] TJ

The first method is preferred.

9.5 Use the appropriate operator to draw text

In most cases, a line of text can be represented in several ways. When deciding among the various methods, try to draw the line using as few operations as possible. Table 9.1 provides guidelines for selecting the appropriate text string operator.

Table 9.1 *Comparison of text string operators*

Use	When...
'	Complete line of text can be drawn together No need for individual character spacings
"	Complete line of text can be drawn together Non-zero character or word spacings on each line No need for individual character spacings
Tj	Multiple text operators per line of text No need for individual character spacings
TJ	Individual character spacings needed

When laying out a line of text with non-default character spacings, such as kerned text, use the **TJ** operator rather than a series of pairs of **Tj** and **Td** operators. For example, both of the following lines produce the same output for the Helvetica Bold Oblique font at a size of 12 points:

```
(A f) Tj 15.64 0 Td (ew w) Tj 28.08 0 Td (ords) Tj
[(A f) 30 (ew w) 50 (ords)] TJ
```

The second method is preferred because it minimizes the size of the file and the number of text operators.

9.6 Use the appropriate operator to position text

The **TD**, **Td**, **Tm**, and **T*** operators each change the location at which subsequent text is drawn. Use each of these operators under different circumstances. Table 9.2 provides guidelines for selecting the appropriate text positioning operator.

Table 9.2 *Comparison of text positioning operators*

Use	When...
Td	Changing only the text location
TD	Changing text location and leading
Tm	Rotating, scaling, or skewing text
T*	Moving to start of next line of text, as defined by the leading

9.7 Remove text clipping

After text has been used as a clipping path through one of the clipping text rendering modes (4–7), the original clipping path must be restored. Restoration of the original clipping path is accomplished using the **q** and **Q** operators to save and subsequently restore the clipping path, respectively.

Neither **q** nor **Q** may appear inside a text object. Save the original clipping path using the **q** operator before beginning the text object in which a new clipping path is set. When you want to restore the original clipping path, the text object must be ended using the **ET** operator. Then, use the **Q** operator to restore the original clipping path. Following this, another text object can be entered if more text is to be drawn.

Example 9.10 illustrates the proper way to save and restore a clipping path when using one of the clipping text rendering modes.

Example 9.10 *Restoring clipping path after using text as clipping path*

```
q
BT
/F13 48 Tf
200 414 Td
%Set clip path
0.25 w
5 Tr
(Clip) Tj
ET
BT
200 450 Td
/F13 6 Tf
0 Tr
6 TL
(ClipClipClipClipClipClipClipClip) '
(ClipClipClipClipClipClipClipClip) '
(ClipClipClipClipClipClipClipClip) '
(ClipClipClipClipClipClipClipClip) '
(ClipClipClipClipClipClipClipClip) '
(ClipClipClipClipClipClipClipClip) '
(ClipClipClipClipClipClipClip) '
(ClipClipClipClipClipClipClip) '
(ClipClipClipClipClipClipClip) '
ET
Q
BT
/F13 12 Tf
175 395 Td
(Default Clipping Restored) Tj
ET
```

Figure 9.1 shows the output produced by this example when F13 is Helvetica Bold Oblique. The presence of the words "Default Clipping Restored" at the bottom of the figure demonstrates that the clipping path has been restored to its previous value.

Figure 9.1 *Restoring clipping path after clipping to text*

9.8 Consider target device resolution

Although text in a PDF file is resolution-independent (unless a document contains bitmapped Type 3 fonts), there are still reasons to consider the resolution of the target device. Text positioning, in particular, may depend on the primary target device.

It is possible to individually position each character in a string using, for example, the **TJ** operator. This allows precise layout of text. However, adjusting the location of each character increases the size of a PDF file because the positioning must be specified by numbers that are otherwise not needed. In addition, drawing text is slower when each character is individually positioned. As mentioned in Section 8.11, "Consider target device resolution," if the primary target is a low-resolution device such as a computer screen, producing a small file and one that draws quickly is generally more important than having extremely precise positioning. If the primary target is an imagesetter, extremely precise positioning is generally the primary concern.

As an example of the choices that can be made, suppose the positions of each character on a 60-character line are adjusted from their normal positions by an amount corresponding to 0.01 pixels on a 72 pixel per inch computer screen. The total adjustment across the entire line is just over half a pixel on the screen. If the document is primarily intended to be viewed on a computer screen, omitting the adjustments would make sense because such a small adjustment is invisible. The result would be a smaller file that can be drawn more quickly. On the other hand, the same adjustment corresponds to 10 pixels on a 1200 pixel per inch imagesetter. If the primary target is such an imagesetter, it may be worthwhile retaining the individual position adjustment. Note that precise text positioning is most important for justified text, where positioning errors are easily detected by users.

CHAPTER **10**

Optimizing Graphics

10.1 Use the appropriate color-setting operator

Use **0 g** to set the fill color to black, rather than the equivalent, but longer, **0 0 0 rg** or **0 0 0 1 k**. Similarly, **0 G** should be used to set the stroke color to black instead of **0 0 0 RG** or **0 0 0 1 K**. In general, if a color contains equal color components, use either **g** or **G**, as appropriate. For example, use **.8 G** instead of **.8 .8 .8 RG**.

10.2 Defer path painting until necessary

When representing graphics in a PDF file, each path segment can be treated as a separate path or a number of segments can be grouped together into a single path. Wherever possible, group segments together into a single path. This reduces the size of the file and improves drawing speed. However, a path should not contain more than approximately 1500 segments. For further information, see Appendix B of the *PostScript Language Reference Manual, Second Edition*.

Because a path can only be filled with a single color and stroked with a single color, line width, miter limit, and line cap style, a new path must be started whenever one or more of these values is changed.

As an illustration, Example 10.1 and Example 10.2 produce identical output, but the technique shown in Example 10.2 is preferred. Note that Example 10.2 still contains two paths. These paths cannot be combined, because they have different stroke colors.

Example 10.1 *Each path segment as a separate path*

```
.5 0 1 RG
100 100 m
100 200 l
S
100 200 m
200 200 l
S
200 200 m
200 100 l
S
200 100 m
100 100 l
S
0 .2 .4 RG
300 300 m
400 300 l
S
```

Example 10.2 *Grouping path segments into a single path*

```
.5 0 1 RG
100 100 m
100 200 l
200 200 l
200 100 l
s
0 .2 .4 RG
300 300 m
400 300 l
S
```

10.3 Take advantage of the closepath operator

The **h** (**closepath**) operator closes the current subpath by drawing a straight segment from the endpoint of the last segment drawn to the first point in the subpath. When the last segment in a path is straight, use the **h** operator to draw the final segment and close the path.

Two inefficient ways of closing a path commonly occur. The first, shown in Example 10.3, uses the **l** operator to draw the final segment, followed by the **h** operator to close the path.

Example 10.3 *Using redundant* l *and* h *operators to close a path inefficiently*

```
100 100 m
100 200 l
200 200 l
200 100 l
100 100 l
h
```

The second, shown in Example 10.4, uses the l operator to draw the final segment of the path.

Example 10.4 *Using the* l *operator to close a path inefficiently*

```
100 100 m
100 200 l
200 200 l
200 100 l
100 100 l
```

Example 10.5 shows the correct way of closing a path with a straight segment, using the h operator.

Example 10.5 *Taking advantage of the* h *operator to close a path*

```
100 100 m
100 200 l
200 200 l
200 100 l
h
```

If the h operator is not used, the appropriate line join will not occur at the juncture of the path's initial and final point.

10.4   Don't close a path more than once

Close a path only one time. Don't use the h operator before a path painting operator that implicitly closes the path: the n, b, f, f* and s operators. In addition, the h operator should not be used with the **re** operator, because the **re** operator produces a path that is already closed.

For example, do not use a sequence as in Example 10.6, because the s operator automatically closes the path before stroking it.

Example 10.6 *Improperly closing a path: multiple path closing operators*

150 240.7 m
253.2 200 l
180.4 150 l
75.4 134.5 l
h
s

Instead, use the sequence:

Example 10.7 *Properly closing a path: single path closing operator*

150 240.7 m
253.2 200 l
180.4 150 l
75.4 134.5 l
s

10.5   Don't draw zero-length lines

When generating graphics from a computer program, it is not uncommon to produce line segments of zero length. Such line segments produce no useful output and should be eliminated before the PDF file is written.

Line segments of zero length may arise when straight line segments are used to approximate a curve. Generally, the programmer wants to make sure that the approximation is close to the actual curve, and so takes small steps in approximating the curve. Occasionally the steps are small enough that they produce segments of zero length after the coordinates have been converted to the format in which they are written to the file. (See Section 8.8, "Limit the precision of real numbers.")

Zero-length line segments may also be generated when making a two-dimensional projection of a three-dimensional object. Lines in the three-dimensional object that go directly into the page have zero length in the two-dimensional projection.

10.6   Make sure drawing is needed

When generating graphics from a computer program, test before writing the graphics to a PDF file to ensure that the graphics actually make new marks on the page and do not simply draw over marks already made.

Redundant graphics typically arise when making a two–dimensional projection of a three–dimensional object. It is possible to end up with several images that lie on top of one another after being projected.

10.7 Take advantage of rectangle and curve operators

Use the **re** operator to draw a rectangle, instead of the corresponding sequence of **m** and **l** operators.

Curves can be drawn in one of two ways; either by approximating the curve with a sequence of straight segments or by using the curve operators present in PDF. Although approximating curves using straight segments is easy, it typically results in a very large amount of data. Use the curve operators (**c**, **v**, **y**) to represent curves in PDF files. Doing so results in a smaller file that can be rendered more quickly.

An algorithm for automatically fitting an arbitrary set of points with a cubic Bézier curve, like those used by PDF, can be found in the book *Graphics Gems*. The algorithm described in *Graphics Gems* begins by assuming the points supplied can be fit by a single cubic Bézier curve, with the two endpoints of the Bézier curve being the first and last data points, and the Bézier control points calculated from the approximate tangents at the endpoints of the supplied data. The algorithm minimizes the sum of the squares of the distances between the data points and the curve being fit by moving the control points. If a satisfactory fit cannot be obtained, the data points are separated into two groups at the point with the greatest distance between the curve being fit and the actual data point, and two separate Bézier curves are fit to the two sets of points. This fitting and splitting is repeated until a satisfactory fit is obtained. See the Bibliography for more information.

10.8 Coalesce operations

Graphics generated by a computer program occasionally contain a group of operations that can be combined into a single operation. These can arise, for example, when a curve is approximated by a series of short straight segments. Significant sections of the curve being approximated may be effectively straight, but the approximation program typically does not realize this and continues to approximate the curve as a sequence of small line segments, instead of combining collinear segments.

For example, the sequence shown in Example 10.8 contains a number of segments that should be combined. Specifically, the first four **l** operators simply draw one straight line segment and should be combined.

Example 10.8 *Portion of a path before coalescing operations*

```
100 100 m
100 101 l
100 102 l
100 103 l
100 104 l
101 105 l
```

The entire sequence can be replaced by the equivalent and more efficient sequence in Example 10.9.

Example 10.9 *Portion of a path after coalescing operations*

```
100 100 m
100 104 l
101 105 l
```

CHAPTER 11

Optimizing Images

Sampled images typically require more memory and take more time to process and draw than any other graphics object element of a page. By carefully choosing an appropriate resolution, number of bits per color component, and compression filter, it is possible to significantly enhance image performance.

11.1 Preprocess images

PDF provides operators that transform and clip images. These operators should be used with care. For example, performance often improves if rotation and skewing of an image is performed before the image is placed in the PDF file, rather than by the PDF viewer application. Similarly, if an image is clipped, it is best to reduce to the image the smallest dimensions possible before placing the image in the PDF file, perhaps eliminating the need for clipping.

11.2 Match image resolution to target device resolution

If a grayscale or color image will primarily be viewed on computer screens (which typically have resolutions between 70–100 pixels per inch) or printed on typical color and monochrome printers (which have resolutions of 300-dpi and default halftone screens of approximately 60 lines per inch), there is no point in producing the image at 300 samples per inch. Most of the information in the higher resolution image will never be seen, the image will contain at least nine times as much data as it needs to (90,000 samples per square inch versus a maximum of 10,000 samples per square inch), and will draw more slowly.

Monochrome images can be stored at higher resolutions of 200- to 300-dpi. This resolution can be achieved on typical printers.

11.3 Use the minimum number of bits per color component

The amount of data needed to represent an image increases as the number of bits per color component increases. This is very important to consider when deciding how many bits per component to use for an image.

If an image requires continuous colors, it might very well need to use 8 bits per color component. However, many graphs, plots, and other types of drawings do not require continuous tone reproduction and are completely satisfactory with a small number of bits per color component.

11.4 Take advantage of indexed color spaces

If an image contains a relatively small number of colors, indexed color spaces can be used to reduce the amount of data needed to represent the image. In an indexed color space, the number of bits needed to represent each sample in an image is determined by the total number of colors in the image rather than by the precision needed to specify a single color.

Most computers currently have displays that support a limited number of colors. For example, it is very common for color displays on the Macintosh computer to provide no more than 256 colors, and many computers running the Microsoft Windows environment provide only 16 colors. On such devices, little loss of image quality will occur if 24-bit color images are replaced by 8-bit indexed color images.

As an example of the compression possible using indexed color spaces, suppose an image contains 256 different colors. Each pixel's color can then be encoded using only 8 bits, regardless of whether the colors in the image are 8-bit grayscale, 24-bit RGB, or 32-bit CMYK. If the colors are 24-bit RGB, using an indexed color space instead of the RGB values would reduce the amount of data needed to represent the image by approximately a factor of three; 24 bits per pixel using an RGB color space versus 8 bits per pixel using an indexed color space. The reduction is not exactly three because the use of an indexed color space requires that a look-up table, containing the list of colors used in the image, be written to the file. For a large image, the size of this lookup table is insignificant compared to the image and can be ignored. For a small image, the size of the look-up table must be included in the calculation. The size of the lookup table can be calculated from the description of indexed color spaces in Section 6.8.5, "Color space resources."

11.5 Use the DeviceGray color space for monochrome images

For a bitmap (monochrome) image, use the **DeviceGray** color space instead of **DeviceRGB**, **DeviceCMYK**, or an indexed color space. In addition, the **BitsPerComponent** attribute for bitmap images should be 1. These settings significantly reduce the amount of data used to represent the image.

Using a different color space or a larger **BitsPerComponent** greatly increases the amount of image data. As an extreme example, a bitmap image represented using a **DeviceCMYK** color space with 8 bits per component contains 32 times as much data as necessary: four color components with 8 bits per component, instead of a single color component with 1 bit per component.

11.6 Use in-line images appropriately

In-line images occupy less disk space and memory than image resources. However, image resources give viewer applications more flexibility in managing memory—the data of an image resource can be read on demand, while an in-line image must be kept in memory together with the rest of a page's contents.

PDF Writer and the Acrobat Distiller application represent images with less than 4K of data as in-line images until a total of 32K of in-line data are present on a page. Once this limit is reached, subsequent images on that page are represented in-line only if they are smaller than 1K.

11.7 Don't compress in-line images unnecessarily

In-line images should not always be compressed and converted to ASCII. Specifically, in-line images should not be compressed if the Contents stream of the page on which the in-line image appears is itself compressed.

Because an in-line image is located completely within the Contents stream of the page, it is automatically passed through the compression and ASCII conversion filters specified for the page's Contents stream. The specification of an additional compression or ASCII conversion filter in the in-line image itself under these circumstances results in the in-line image being compressed and converted to ASCII twice. This does not result in additional compression and slows down the decoding of the image.

11.8   Choose the appropriate filters

The selection of filters for image streams can be confusing, although a few relatively simple rules can greatly simplify the task. In PDF files, filters compress data or encode binary data as ASCII. All data in a PDF file must be 7-bit ASCII, so binary-to-ASCII conversion filters must be used to record binary data.

The order of filters specified when data is decoded must be the opposite of the order in which the filters were applied when the data was encoded. For example, if data is encoded first using LZW and then by ASCII base-85, during decoding the ASCII base-85 filter must be used before the LZW decoding filter. In a stream object, the decoding filters and the order in which they are applied are specified by the **Filter** key. The example would appear as:

/Filter [/ASCII85Decode /LZWDecode]

Any time binary data is stored in a PDF file, the last encoding filter applied (and therefore the first decoding filter specified in the stream's **Filter** key) must be one of the two binary-to-ASCII conversion filters supported by PDF: ASCII hexadecimal and ASCII base-85. Between these two, the ASCII base-85 encoding, which is decoded by the ASCII85Decode filter, is preferred because it produces a much smaller expansion in the amount of data than ASCII hexadecimal encoding does.

PDF supports several compression filters that reduce the size of data written into a PDF file. The compression filters can be broken down into two classes: lossless and lossy. A lossless filter is one in which the process of encoding and decoding results in no loss of information: the decoded data is bit-by-bit identical to the original data. For a lossy filter, the process of encoding and decoding results in a loss of information: the decoded data is not bit-by-bit identical to the original data. Lossy filters can be used when the resulting loss of information is not visually significant. The JPEG filter supported by PDF is a lossy filter.

JPEG encoding, which can be decoded by the DCTDecode filter, provides very significant compression of color and grayscale images, but because it is a lossy compression it is not appropriate in all circumstances. Screenshots, in particular, are often unacceptable when JPEG encoded. This happens because each pixel in a screenshot is usually significant, and the loss or alteration of just a few pixels can drastically alter the appearance of the screenshot.

Figure 11.1 shows the effect of JPEG encoding on screenshots. The images shown in the figure are magnified by a factor of two to show the changes due to the compression. The 8×8 pixel blocks used in JPEG encoding appear clearly in the pattern inside the icon encoded using a high JPEG compression. The definitions of high, medium, and low JPEG compression are those used by the Acrobat Distiller program. The amount of data in the image from which the figure is taken is: 153,078 bytes with no JPEG encoding, 28,396 bytes with low compression JPEG encoding, 16,944 bytes with medium compression JPEG encoding, and 10,679 bytes with high compression JPEG encoding. All these sizes are for the data in the format in which it appears in the PDF file; that is, after it has been ASCII base-85 encoded.

Figure 11.1 *Effect of JPEG encoding on a screenshot*

No JPEG compression

Low JPEG compression

Medium JPEG compression

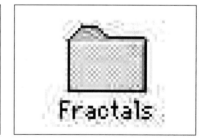

High JPEG compression

Unlike screenshots, the effect of JPEG encoding on continuous-tone images is typically acceptable, particularly when high compression is not demanded. Figure 11.2 illustrates the effect. The image shown in the figure has been magnified by a factor of two to make the effect of JPEG encoding more readily observable. The version obtained using high compression clearly shows the 8×8 pixel blocks used in JPEG encoding. As in the previous example, the definitions of high, medium, and low JPEG compression are those used by the Acrobat Distiller program, and the sizes shown are for the data in the format in which it appears in the PDF file; that is, after it has been ASCII base-85 encoded.

Figure 11.2 *Effect of JPEG encoding on a continuous-tone image*

No JPEG compression; 20,707 bytes *Low JPEG compression; 7,717 bytes*

Medium JPEG compression; 3,470 bytes *High JPEG compression; 1,997 bytes*

In addition to JPEG, PDF supports several lossless compression filters that may be used for images. Guidelines for selecting among them are summarized in Table 11.1.

Table 11.1 *Comparison of compression filters for images*

Use	*When...*
DCTDecode	Image is grayscale or color Decompressed image doesn't need to be bit-by-bit identical to original image
CCITTFaxDecode	Image is monochrome (bitmap) Group 4 encoding should be used unless the application generating the file does not support Group 4 encoding
RunLengthDecode	Image contains many groups of identical bytes, such as an 8-bit grayscale image with many areas of same gray level. Should rarely be used
LZWDecode	Images that cannot use **DCTDecode** and that do not compress well using either CCITT or run length encoding

CHAPTER **12**

Clipping and Blends

Clipping restricts the areas on a page where marks can be made. It is similar to using a stencil when painting or airbrushing—a stencil with one or more holes in it is placed on a page. As long as the stencil remains in place, paint only reaches the page through the holes in the stencil. After the stencil is removed, paint can again be applied anywhere on the page. More than one stencil may be used in the production of a single page, and if a second stencil is added before the first one is removed, paint only reaches the page where there are holes in *both* stencils.

Similarly, in producing a PDF page, one or more clipping paths may be used. If a clipping path is not removed before a second clipping path is applied, the resulting clipping path is the intersection of the two paths.

Clipping paths may be specified in two distinct ways: paths and text. These provide clipping that affects all subsequent marking operations until the clipping path is explicitly changed. An example of each type of clipping is provided in the following sections.

Note   *Whenever a clipping path is no longer needed, the default clipping path should be restored, as described in Section 8.4, "Remove unnecessary clipping paths."*

Image masks do not provide clipping as paths and text do, but they can be thought of as specifying a bitmap clipping template that is placed on the page, painted with a color, and then immediately removed. The differences between images and image masks are discussed.

Often, page descriptions contain *blends*, smooth changes of color used as a background or to fill an object. Because blends typically fill objects, and clipping is needed in order to accomplish this, blends are also described in this chapter. A useful way to produce blends using images is provided.

12.1 Clipping to a path

As described in Section 7.5.3, "Path clipping operators," the **W** and **W***
operators can make any path a clipping path. To do this, insert the
operator between the path segment operators and one of the path
painting operators described in Section 7.5.2, "Path painting
operators."

Figure 12.1 shows the effect of clipping to a region in the shape of a
four-pointed star. In the figure, the graphics are shown with and
without the star as a clipping path. To draw the figure, the star is first
stroked and set to be the current clipping path. A series of lines is then
drawn through the star, and the points of the star are filled using arcs.

Figure 12.1 *Clipping to a path*

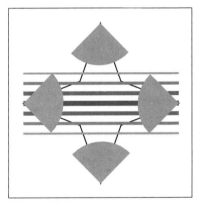 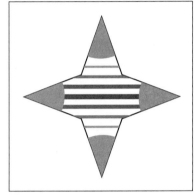

Without clipping to star   *With clipping to star*

Note   *When a path is stroked and used as the current clipping path, remember
        that the stroke extends half the line width on each side of the path, while
        subsequent drawing is clipped to the path itself. Because of this, subsequent
        clipped drawing operations can draw over the "inner half" of the stroke.*

The PDF operations needed to produce this output are shown in
Example 12.1. The star is first drawn using a series of **l** operators. It is set
to be a clipping path using the **W** operator and stroked using the **s**
operator. Next, a series of lines is drawn across the star using the **m** and
l operators. The lines have different gray levels (set by the **G** operator)
and line widths (set by the **w** operator). Because each line has a
different width and color, each must be stroked (using the **S** operator)
individually. To generate the non-clipped portion of the figure, the only
change made to the PDF files was to remove the **W** operator.

Example 12.1 *Clipping to a path*

```
%Draw outline of star
391 392 m
370 450 l
311 472 l
370 494 l
391 552 l
412 494 l
471 472 l
412 450 l
W
s
%Draw lines
.6 G 2 w 311 502 m 471 502 l S
.5 G 3 w 311 492 m 471 492 l S
.4 G 4 w 311 482 m 471 482 l S
.3 G 5 w 311 472 m 471 472 l S
.4 G 4 w 311 462 m 471 462 l S
.5 G 3 w 311 452 m 471 452 l S
.6 G 2 w 311 442 m 471 442 l S
%Draw and fill circles on endpoints
0.6 g
340 443 m
357 460 357 486 341 502 c
311 472 l
f
421 422 m
405 438 379 438 362 421 c
391 392 l
f
442 501 m
425 484 425 458 441 442 c
471 472 l
f
361 522 m
377 506 403 506 420 523 c
391 552 l
f
```

12.2 Clipping to text

Several of the text rendering modes described in Section 7.6.6, "Text rendering mode" allow text to be used as a clipping path. In particular, modes 4 through 7 can be used to clip subsequent drawing to the shapes of one or more characters.

Figure 12.2 shows the word "and" used as a clipping path. The word is first drawn as stroked and clipped text. Following this, a series of lines containing various ampersands is drawn on top of the word. Only those ampersands contained inside the clipping path defined by the word are visible. The font used for the word "and" is Poetica™ Chancery III. The font used for the ampersands is Poetica Ampersands.

Figure 12.2 *Using text as a clipping path*

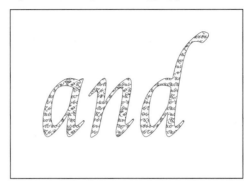

Example 12.2 shows the page description used to produce Figure 12.2. In the example, the font named F6 is Poetica Ampersands and the font named F24 is Poetica Chancery III.

Example 12.2 *Using text as a clipping path*

```
BT
100 500 Td
%Draw the word "and", stroke it and use it as a clipping path
/F24 144 Tf
0.25 w
5 Tr
(and) Tj
ET
BT
%Select Poetica Ampersands font
/F6 6 Tf
100 615 Td
0 Tr
6 TL
%Draw lines of ampersands
(aAbBcCdDeEfFgGhHiIjJkKlLmMnNoOpPqQrRsStTuU) '
(vVwWxXyYzZ123456aAbBcCdDeEfFgGhHiIjJkKlLmMnNoO) '
(pPqQrRsStTuUvVwWxXyYzZ123456aAbBcCdDeEfFgGhH)'
(jJkKlLmMnNoOpPqQrRsStTuUvVwWxXyYzZ123456) '
(aAbBcCdDeEfFgGhHiIjJkKlLmMnNoOpPqQrRsStTuU) '
(vVwWxXyYzZ123456aAbBcCdDeEfFgGhHiIjJkKlLmMnNoO) '
(pPqQrRsStTuUvVwWxXyYzZ123456aAbBcCdDeEfFgGhH) '
```

```
(jJkKlLmMnNoOpPqQrRsStTuUvVwWxXyYzZ123456) '
(aAbBcCdDeEfFgGhHiIjJkKlLmMnNoOpPqQrRsStTuU) '
(vVwWxXyYzZ123456aAbBcCdDeEfFgGhHiIjJkKlLmMnNoO) '
(pPqQrRsStTuUvVwWxXyYzZ123456aAbBcCdDeEfFgGhH) '
(jJkKlLmMnNoOpPqQrRsStTuUvVwWxXyYzZ123456) '
(aAbBcCdDeEfFgGhHiIjJkKlLmMnNoOpPqQrRsStTuU) '
(vVwWxXyYzZ123456aAbBcCdDeEfFgGhHiIjJkKlLmMnNoO) '
(pPqQrRsStTuUvVwWxXyYzZ123456aAbBcCdDeEfFgGhH) '
(jJkKlLmMnNoOpPqQrRsStTuUvVwWxXyYzZ123456) '
(aAbBcCdDeEfFgGhHiIjJkKlLmMnNoOpPqQrRsStTuU) '
(vVwWxXyYzZ123456aAbBcCdDeEfFgGhHiIjJkKlLmMnNoO) '
(pPqQrRsStTuUvVwWxXyYzZ123456aAbBcCdDeEfFgGhH) '
(jJkKlLmMnNoOpPqQrRsStTuUvVwWxXyYzZ123456) '
ET
```

After beginning a text object by using the **BT** operator, the point at
which text will be drawn is set using the **Td** operator. Following this,
the font (named F24) and the size (144 points) are set using the **Tf**
operator, the linewidth for the stroke is set to 0.25 units using the **w**
operator, and the stroked clipping text rendering mode (mode 5) is
selected using the **Tr** operator. The word "and" is then drawn using the
Tj operator. Next, the text object is ended using the **ET** operator. This is
necessary in order to draw text using a different rendering mode.
Following this, another text object is started, the ampersand font
(named F6) and the size (6 points) are set, the position where text will
be drawn is moved, the filled text rendering mode (mode 0) is selected,
and the line leading is set to 6 points using the **TL** operator. Finally,
the ampersands are drawn by a series of ' operators, and the text
object ends.

12.3   Image masks

Although image masks do not provide clipping as described above, they
can be thought of as operating as follows: a bitmap image defines the
clipping path, where 1s and 0s are considered to be holes and masks.
The rectangle containing the bitmap is painted with the current fill
color. Immediately following this, the bitmap-derived clipping path is
removed.

Image masks differ from images in two ways. First, when an image is
drawn, all pixels in the rectangle of the image are painted. In an image
mask, only the pixels under holes in the mask are painted; all other
pixels are left unchanged. Second, the colors in which an image is
painted are encoded inside the image itself, while an image mask is
painted using the current fill color at the time the image mask is drawn.
Because of this, an image mask may appear in different colors each time
it is drawn.

As described in Section 6.8.6, "XObject resources," the structure of an image mask differs from that of an image in several ways. First, an image mask must have only one bit per color component. Second, an image mask must not contain a color space specification, while an image must. Third, the image mask dictionary must contain the **ImageMask** key with a value of *true*. For both images and image masks, the array specified as the value of the **Decode** key in the image can be used to choose whether bits containing 1s or bits containing 0s are considered to be set.

Figure 12.3 shows examples of images and image masks. The examples also illustrate how the decode array can be used to invert the image.

Figure 12.3 *Images and image masks*

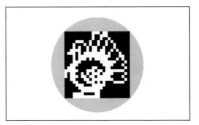

Image

Inverted image

Image mask

Inverted image mask

Example 12.3 shows the relevant sections from the PDF file used to produce the figure. Because the only difference between the PDF files used to draw each of the four examples is in the image object itself, all the drawing operations are common. The **0.6 g** operation appearing just before the image or image mask is drawn has an effect only when the object being drawn is an image mask, not an image. The example shows the operations used to draw the image mask portion of the figure. To produce the image portion of the figure, the line **/ImageMask true** was replaced with the line **/ColorSpace /DeviceGray**. For the inverted image and inverted image mask, the line **/Decode [1 0]** was added to the dictionary of the image or image mask.

Example 12.3 *Images and image masks*

```
3 0 obj
<<
/Type /Page
/Parent 4 0 R
/MediaBox [ 53 470 198 616 ]
/Resources << /XObject << /Im0 60 0 R >>
/ProcSet [ /PDF /ImageC ] >>
/Contents 23 0 R
>>
endobj
23 0 obj
<< /Length 205 >>
stream
%Draw a circle and fill it
0.8 g
126 472 m
165 472 197 504 197 543 c
197 582 165 614 126 614 c
87 614 55 582 55 543 c
55 504 87 472 126 472 c
f
%Draw image or mask
q
100 0 0 100 76 493.2 cm
.6 g
/Im0 Do
Q
endstream
endobj
60 0 obj
<< /Type /XObject
/Subtype /Image
/Name /Im0
/Width 24
/Height 23
/BitsPerComponent 1
/Filter /ASCIIHexDecode
/Length 162
/ImageMask true
>>
stream
003b00 002700 002480 0e4940
114920 14b220 3cb650 75fe88
17ff8c 175f14 1c07e2 3803c4
703182 f8edfc b2bbc2 bb6f84
31bfc2 18ea3c 0e3e00 07fc00
03f800 1e1800 1ff800>
endstream
endobj
```

12.4 Blends

Several approaches may be used to produce blends. One alternative is to draw path segments such as rectangles, lines, and arcs adjacent to each other, each having a slightly different color. This method can result in large files and is slow to draw. Using images is often a much better method for producing blends.

Blends made using images usually occupy much less space in a PDF file. Images also have the advantage that they can be filled with arbitrary sequences of colors to provide arbitrary blends, and they can be easily stretched, rotated, and skewed in order to provide a variety of blend effects from a single image. In addition, the colors in an image can vary arbitrarily from sample to sample, allowing the production of effects that are difficult or impossible using path segment operators.

Using an image as a blend involves several steps:

1. Create the image containing the blend.

2. Draw the shape to be filled with the blend and make it the current clipping path.

3. Scale and translate the image using the **cm** operator so that it completely fills the shape.

4. Draw the image using the **Do** operator.

5. Remove the clipping path created in Step 2 so that any subsequent drawing is not restricted to the shape of the object that was filled with the blend.

To create a linear blend in which the color inside an object varies smoothly from top to bottom, only a one-sample-wide image is needed, with as many rows in the image as there are to be steps in the blend. Each sample in the image is given the color of the corresponding band in the blend. For example, to create a four-step grayscale blend that goes from medium gray to black, create an image with a **Width** of 1, a **Height** of 4, and a ColorSpace of DeviceGray. Set the BitsPerComponent as needed. Suppose you set it to 8. The image data contains the colors to be used in the blend. In this example, you might set them to 00, 20, 40, and 60 hexadecimal.

Now that this image has been created, it can be rotated to provide other blends. For example, to obtain a four-step horizontal blend instead of a vertical blend, the image need only be rotated by 90 degrees by setting the appropriate matrix (using the **cm** operator) before drawing the image.

Figure 12.4 illustrates the use of an image to produce a linear blend. The example consists of a circle, stroked and used as a clipping path for a 32-step vertical gray blend. A second blend is used inside the letter. This 27-step blend runs from light pink at the top to deep red at the bottom. The blend is tilted 30 degrees, so that the lines of constant color are approximately parallel to the stem coming off the left side of the letter "L".

Note *The example blends in this chapter use a relatively small number of steps. This is done only to minimize the size of the examples. Blends of 256 steps, which generally provide smooth blends, can be used without a significant performance degradation.*

Figure 12.4 *Using an image to produce a linear blend*

The relevant sections from the PDF file used to produce the figure are shown in Example 12.4. The example is explained in the following paragraphs.

Example 12.4 *Using images as blends*

```
3 0 obj
<<
/Type /Page
/Parent 4 0 R
/MediaBox [ 0 0 612 792 ]
/Resources << /Font << /F39 7 0 R >>
/XObject << /Im0 10 0 R /Im1 11 0 R >>
/ProcSet [ /PDF /Text /ImageC ] >>
/Contents 6 0 R
>>
endobj
6 0 obj
<< /Length 383 >>
stream
%Draw circle, use it as a clipping path
q
126 472 m
165 472 197 504 197 543 c
197 582 165 614 126 614 c
87 614 55 582 55 543 c
55 504 87 472 126 472 c
W
s
%Draw image inside circle
-150 0 0 -150 200 620 cm
/Im0 Do
Q
%Draw character, stroke it and use it as a clipping path
q
BT
85 510 Td
/F39 144 Tf
0.25 w
5 Tr
(L) Tj
ET
%Draw image inside text
147 85 -50 86.7 45 420 cm
/Im1 Do
Q
endstream
endobj
10 0 obj
<< /Type /XObject
/Subtype /Image
/Name /Im0
/Width 1
/Height 32
```

```
/BitsPerComponent 8
/ColorSpace /DeviceGray
/Filter /ASCIIHexDecode
 /Length 97 >>
stream
ff f8 ef e8 df d8 cf c8 bf b8 af a8 9f 98 8f 88
7f 78 6f 68 5f 58 4f 48 3f 38 2f 28 1f 18 0f 08>
endstream
endobj
11 0 obj
<< /Type /XObject
/Subtype /Image
/Name /Im1
 /Width 1
 /Height 27
/BitsPerComponent 8
/ColorSpace /DeviceRGB
/Filter /ASCIIHexDecode
/Length 190 >>
stream
ffd0d0 ffc8c8 ffc0c0 ffb8b8 ffb0b0 ffa8a8 ffa0a0 ff9898 ff9090 ff8888
ff8080 ff7878 ff7070 ff6868 ff6060 ff5858 ff5050 ff4848 ff4040 ff3838
ff3030 ff2828 ff2020 ff1818 ff1010 ff0808 ff0000>
endstream
endobj
```

Object number 3 is the Page object, and is included to show the Resources dictionary, containing the mapping between image and font names used in the page contents, and the objects which are the fonts and images. In addition, the dictionary contains a list of the procsets needed to print this page.

Object number 6 is the page contents. The graphics state is first saved using the **q** operator, in order to be able to restore the original clipping path after drawing the circle and filling it with a blend. Next, the circle is drawn using four Bézier curve segments (the **c** operators), set to be the clipping path using the **W** operator, and stroked using the **s** operator. Following this, the **cm** operator is used to translate and scale the image so that it fills the circle, and the gray blend (named Im0) is drawn using the **Do** operator. Next, the original clipping path is restored using the **Q** operator, and this state saved again, for restoration after using a clipping mode to fill the text.

The text is positioned using the **Td** operator, and the font (named F39, which in the example is Poetica Initial Swash Capitals) and size (144 points) are set using the **Tf** operator. The font object and other related objects are not included in the section shown from the example file. The text rendering mode is set to stroke the text and use it as the clipping path (mode 5) using the **Tr** operator. The text is drawn using the **Tj** operator, and the text object ended. The transformation matrix is again set to scale the image that is to be used as the blend filling the letter. In addition to scaling the image, the matrix used produces a 30-degree rotation to provide a diagonal blend. The image used as the colored blend (named Im1) is drawn, and the initial graphics state restored.

Because the drawing and filling of the text are the last operations in the contents of this particular page, it is not necessary to save the graphics state before entering the text object and to restore the graphics state after drawing the blend. The saving and restoring is included in this example as a reminder that the graphics state must be restored before any subsequent drawing.

Images may be used to produce other blends, such as the square blend shown in Figure 12.5. The blend shown in the figure is a 16-step grayscale blend. Radial blends, in which the bands of constant color are circles, and other arbitrarily complicated blends can also be produced using images.

Figure 12.5 *Using an image to produce a square blend*

The image used to produce the blend is shown in Example 12.5. It is a 31×31 sample grayscale image, with 8 bits per sample.

Example 12.5 *Image used to produce a grayscale square blend*

```
<< /Type /XObject /Subtype /Image /Name /Im0 /Width 31 /Height 31
/BitsPerComponent 8
/ColorSpace /DeviceGray /Filter /ASCIIHexDecode /Length 1954 >>
stream
0000000000000000000000000000000000000000000000000000000000000
00101010101010101010101010101010101010101010101010101010101000
00102020202020202020202020202020202020202020202020202020201000
00102030303030303030303030303030303030303030303030303030201000
00102030404040404040404040404040404040404040404040404030201000
00102030405050505050505050505050505050505050505050504030201000
00102030405060606060606060606060606060606060606060604030201000
00102030405060707070707070707070707070707070707070604030201000
00102030405060708080808080808080808080808080808070604030201000
00102030405060708090909090909090909090909090909080704060504030201000
00102030405060708090a0a0a0a0a0a0a0a0a0a090807060504030201000
00102030405060708090a0b0b0b0b0b0b0b0b0b0a090807060504030201000
00102030405060708090a0b0c0c0c0c0c0c0c0b0a090807060504030201000
00102030405060708090a0b0c0d0d0d0d0d0c0b0a090807060504030201000
00102030405060708090a0b0c0d0e0e0e0d0c0b0a090807060504030201000
00102030405060708090a0b0c0d0e0f0e0d0c0b0a090807060504030201000
00102030405060708090a0b0c0d0e0e0e0d0c0b0a090807060504030201000
00102030405060708090a0b0c0d0d0d0d0d0c0b0a090807060504030201000
00102030405060708090a0b0c0c0c0c0c0c0c0b0a090807060504030201000
00102030405060708090a0b0b0b0b0b0b0b0b0b0a090807060504030201000
00102030405060708090a0a0a0a0a0a0a0a0a0a090807060504030201000
00102030405060708090909090909090909090909090909080704060504030201000
00102030405060708080808080808080808080808080808070604030201000
00102030405060707070707070707070707070707070707070604030201000
00102030405060606060606060606060606060606060606060604030201000
00102030405050505050505050505050505050505050505050504030201000
00102030404040404040404040404040404040404040404040404030201000
00102030303030303030303030303030303030303030303030303030201000
00102020202020202020202020202020202020202020202020202020201000
00101010101010101010101010101010101010101010101010101010101000
0000000000000000000000000000000000000000000000000000000000000>
endstream
```

Example PDF Files

A.1   Minimal PDF file

Although the PDF file shown in this example does not draw anything, it is almost the minimum PDF file possible. It is not strictly the minimum acceptable file because it contains an Outlines object, a Contents object, and a Resources dictionary with a ProcSet resource. These objects were included to make this file useful as a starting point for developing test files. The objects present in this file are listed in Table A.1.

Note   *When using this file as a starting point for creating other files, remember to update the ProcSet resource as needed (see Section 6.8.1, "ProcSet resources.") Also, remember that the cross-reference table entries may need to have a trailing blank (see Section 5.4, "Cross-reference table.")*

Table A.1 *Objects in empty example*

Object number	Object type
1	Catalog
2	Outlines
3	Pages
4	Page
5	Contents
6	ProcSet array

Example A.1 *Minimal PDF file*

```
%PDF-1.0
1 0 obj
<<
/Type /Catalog
/Pages 3 0 R
/Outlines 2 0 R
>>
endobj
2 0 obj
<<
/Type /Outlines
/Count 0
>>
endobj
3 0 obj
<<
/Type /Pages
/Count 1
/Kids [ 4 0 R ]
>>
endobj
4 0 obj
<<
/Type /Page
/Parent 3 0 R
/Resources << /ProcSet 6 0 R >>
/MediaBox [ 0 0 612 792 ]
/Contents 5 0 R
>>
endobj
5 0 obj
<< /Length 35 >>
stream
%place page marking operators here
endstream
endobj
6 0 obj
[ /PDF ]
endobj
xref
0 7
0000000000 65535 f
0000000009 00000 n
0000000074 00000 n
0000000120 00000 n
0000000179 00000 n
0000000300 00000 n
0000000384 00000 n
```

```
trailer
<<
/Size 7
/Root 1 0 R
>>
startxref
408
%%EOF
```

A.2 Simple text string

This PDF file is the classic "Hello World." It displays a single line of text containing that string. The string is displayed in 24-point Helvetica. Because Helvetica is one of the base 14 fonts, no font descriptor is needed. This example illustrates the use of fonts and several text-related PDF operators. The objects contained in the file are listed in Table A.2.

Table A.2 *Objects in "Hello World" example*

Object number	Object type
1	Catalog
2	Outlines
3	Pages
4	Page
5	Contents
6	ProcSet array
7	Font (Type 1 font)

Example A.2 *PDF file for simple text example*

```
%PDF-1.0
1 0 obj
<<
/Type /Catalog
/Pages 3 0 R
/Outlines 2 0 R
>>
endobj
2 0 obj
<<
/Type /Outlines
/Count 0
>>
```

```
endobj
3 0 obj
<<
/Type /Pages
/Count 1
/Kids [ 4 0 R ]
>>
endobj
4 0 obj
<<
/Type /Page
/Parent 3 0 R
/Resources << /Font << /F1 7 0 R >> /ProcSet 6 0 R >>
/MediaBox [ 0 0 612 792 ]
/Contents 5 0 R
>>
endobj
5 0 obj
<< /Length 44 >>
stream
BT
/F1 24 Tf
100 100 Td (Hello World) Tj
ET
endstream
endobj
6 0 obj
[ /PDF /Text ]
endobj
7 0 obj
<<
/Type /Font
/Subtype /Type1
/Name /F1
/BaseFont /Helvetica
/Encoding /MacRomanEncoding
>>
endobj
xref
0 8
0000000000 65535 f
0000000009 00000 n
0000000074 00000 n
0000000120 00000 n
0000000179 00000 n
0000000322 00000 n
0000000415 00000 n
0000000445 00000 n
trailer
<<
```

```
/Size 8
/Root 1 0 R
>>
startxref
553
%%EOF
```

A.3 Simple graphics

This PDF file draws a thin black line segment, a thick black dashed line segment, a filled and stroked rectangle, and a filled and stroked Bézier curve. The file contains comments showing the various operations. The objects present in this file are listed in Table A.3.

Table A.3 *Objects in graphics example*

Object number	Object type
1	Catalog
2	Outlines
3	Pages
4	Page
5	Contents
6	ProcSets

Example A.3 *PDF file for simple graphics example*

```
%PDF-1.0
1 0 obj
<<
/Type /Catalog
/Pages 3 0 R
/Outlines 2 0 R
>>
endobj
2 0 obj
<<
/Type /Outlines
/Count 0
>>
endobj
3 0 obj
<<
/Type /Pages
/Count 1
/Kids [ 4 0 R ]
>>
endobj
```

```
4 0 obj
<<
/Type /Page
/Parent 3 0 R
/Resources << /ProcSet 6 0 R >>
/MediaBox [ 0 0 612 792 ]
/Contents 5 0 R
>>
endobj
5 0 obj
<< /Length 604 >>
stream
% Draw a black line segment, using the default line width
150 250 m
150 350 l
S
% Draw thicker, dashed line segment
150 250 m
4 w  %set a linewidth of 4 points
[4 6] 0 d  %set a dash pattern with 4 units on, 6 units off
400 250 l
S
[ ] 0 d  %reset dash pattern to a solid line
1 w %reset linewidth to 1 unit
%Draw a rectangle, 1 unit light blue border, filled with red
200 200 m
.5 .75 1 rg %light blue for fill color
1 0 0 RG  %red for stroke color
200 300 50 75 re
B
%Draw a curve using a Bézier curve, filled with gray and with a colored border
.5 .1 .2 RG
0.7 g
300 300 m
300 400 400 400 400 300 c
b
endstream
endobj
6 0 obj
[ /PDF ]
endobj
xref
0 7
0000000000 65535 f
0000000009 00000 n
0000000074 00000 n
0000000120 00000 n
0000000179 00000 n
0000000300 00000 n
0000000954 00000 n
```

```
trailer
<<
/Size 7
/Root 1 0 R
>>
startxref
978
%%EOF
```

A.4 Pages tree

This example is a fragment of a PDF file, illustrating the structure of the Pages tree for a large document. It contains the Pages objects for a 62-page file. The structure of the Pages tree for this example is shown in Figure A.1. In the figure, the numbers are object numbers corresponding to the objects in the PDF document fragment contained in Example A.4.

Figure A.1 *Pages tree for 62-page document example*

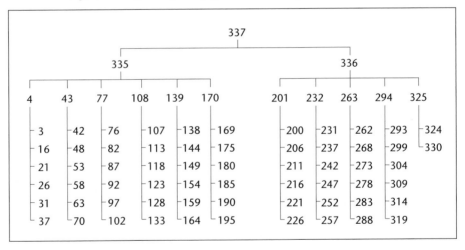

Example A.4 *Pages tree for a document containing 62 pages*

```
337 0 obj
<<
/Kids [335 0 R 336 0 R]
/Count 62
/Type /Pages
>>
endobj
```

```
335 0 obj
<<
/Kids [4 0 R 43 0 R 77 0 R 108 0 R 139 0 R 170 0 R ]
/Count 36
/Type /Pages
/Parent 337 0 R
>>
endobj

336 0 obj
<<
/Kids [201 0 R 232 0 R 263 0 R 294 0 R 325 0 R ]
/Count 26
/Type /Pages
/Parent 337 0 R
>>
endobj

4 0 obj
<<
/Kids [3 0 R 16 0 R 21 0 R 26 0 R 31 0 R 37 0 R ]
/Count 6
/Type /Pages
/Parent 335 0 R
>>
endobj

43 0 obj
<<
/Kids [42 0 R 48 0 R 53 0 R 58 0 R 63 0 R 70 0 R ]
/Count 6
/Type /Pages
/Parent 335 0 R
>>
endobj

77 0 obj
<<
/Kids [76 0 R 82 0 R 87 0 R 92 0 R 97 0 R 102 0 R ]
/Count 6
/Type /Pages
/Parent 335 0 R
>>
endobj

108 0 obj
<<
/Kids [107 0 R 113 0 R 118 0 R 123 0 R 128 0 R 133 0 R ]
/Count 6
/Type /Pages
```

```
/Parent 335 0 R
>>
endobj

139 0 obj
<<
/Kids [138 0 R 144 0 R 149 0 R 154 0 R 159 0 R 164 0 R ]
/Count 6
/Type /Pages
/Parent 335 0 R
>>
endobj

170 0 obj
<<
/Kids [169 0 R 175 0 R 180 0 R 185 0 R 190 0 R 195 0 R ]
/Count 6
/Type /Pages
/Parent 335 0 R
>>
endobj

201 0 obj
<<
/Kids [200 0 R 206 0 R 211 0 R 216 0 R 221 0 R 226 0 R ]
/Count 6
/Type /Pages
/Parent 336 0 R
>>
endobj

232 0 obj
<<
/Kids [231 0 R 237 0 R 242 0 R 247 0 R 252 0 R 257 0 R ]
/Count 6
/Type /Pages
/Parent 336 0 R
>>
endobj

263 0 obj
<<
/Kids [262 0 R 268 0 R 273 0 R 278 0 R 283 0 R 288 0 R ]
/Count 6
/Type /Pages
/Parent 336 0 R
>>
endobj
```

```
294 0 obj
<<
/Kids [293 0 R 299 0 R 304 0 R 309 0 R 314 0 R 319 0 R ]
/Count 6
/Type /Pages
/Parent 336 0 R
>>
endobj

325 0 obj
<<
/Kids [324 0 R 330 0 R ]
/Count 2
/Type /Pages
/Parent 336 0 R
>>
endobj
```

A.5 Outline

This section from a PDF file illustrates the structure of an outline tree with six entries. Example A.5 shows the outline with all entries open, as illustrated in Figure A.2.

Figure A.2 *Example of outline with six items, all open*

Onscreen appearance	Object number	Count
Document	21	6
	22	4
Section 1	25	0
Section 2	26	1
Subsection 1	27	0
Section 3	28	0
Summary	29	0

Example A.5 *Six entry outline, all items open*

```
21 0 obj
<<
/Count 6
/Type /Outlines
/First 22 0 R
/Last 29 0 R
>>
endobj
```

```
22 0 obj
<<
/Parent 21 0 R
/Dest [ 3 0 R /Top 0 792 0 ]
/Title (Document)
/Next 29 0 R
/First 25 0 R
/Last 28 0 R
/Count 4
>>
endobj

25 0 obj
<<
/Dest [ 3 0 R /FitR -38 255 650 792 ]
/Parent 22 0 R
/Title (Section 1)
/Next 26 0 R
>>
endobj

26 0 obj
<<
/Dest [ 3 0 R /FitR -38 255 650 792 ]
/Prev 25 0 R
/Next 28 0 R
/Parent 22 0 R
/Title (Section 2)
/First 27 0 R
/Last 27 0 R
/Count 1
>>
endobj

27 0 obj
<<
/Dest [ 3 0 R /FitR 65498 255 650 792 ]
/Parent 26 0 R
/Title (Subsection 1)
>>
endobj

28 0 obj
<<
/Dest [ 3 0 R /FitR 3 255 622 792 ]
/Prev 26 0 R
/Parent 22 0 R
/Title (Section 3)
>>
endobj
```

```
29 0 obj
<<
/Prev 22 0 R
/Parent 21 0 R
/Dest [ 3 0 R /FitR 3 255 622 792 ]
/Title (Summary)
>>
endobj
```

Example A.6 is the same as Example A.5, except that one of the outline items has been closed. The outline appears as shown in Figure A.3.

Figure A.3 *Example of outline with six items, five of which are open*

Onscreen appearance	Object number	Count
Document	21	5
	22	3
Section 1	25	0
Section 2	26	−1
Section 3	28	0
Summary	29	0

Example A.6 *Six entry outline, five entries open*

```
21 0 obj
<<
/Count 5
/Type /Outlines
/First 22 0 R
/Last 29 0 R
>>
endobj

22 0 obj
<<
/Parent 21 0 R
/Dest [ 3 0 R /Top 0 792 0 ]
/Title (Document)
/Next 29 0 R
/First 25 0 R
/Last 28 0 R
/Count 3
>>
endobj
```

```
25 0 obj
<<
/Dest [ 3 0 R /FitR -38 255 650 792 ]
/Parent 22 0 R
/Title (Section 1)
/Next 26 0 R
>>
endobj

26 0 obj
<<
/Dest [ 3 0 R /FitR -38 255 650 792 ]
/Prev 25 0 R
/Next 28 0 R
/Parent 22 0 R
/Title (Section 2)
/First 27 0 R
/Last 27 0 R
/Count -1
>>
endobj

27 0 obj
<<
/Dest [ 3 0 R /FitR 65498 255 650 792 ]
/Parent 26 0 R
/Title (Subsection 1)
>>
endobj

28 0 obj
<<
/Dest [ 3 0 R /FitR 3 255 622 792 ]
/Prev 26 0 R
/Parent 22 0 R
/Title (Section 3)
>>
endobj

29 0 obj
<<
/Prev 22 0 R
/Parent 21 0 R
/Dest [ 3 0 R /FitR 3 255 622 792 ]
/Title (Summary)
>>
endobj
```

A.6   Updated file

This example shows the structure of a PDF file as it is updated several times; multiple body sections, cross-reference sections, and trailers. In addition, it illustrates the fact that once an object ID has been assigned to an object, it keeps the ID until it is deleted, even if the object is altered. Finally, it illustrates the re-use of cross-reference entries for objects that have been deleted, along with the incrementing of the generation number after an object has been deleted.

The original file is that used in Section A.1, "Minimal PDF file." This file is not shown again here. First, four text annotations are added and the file saved. Next, the text of one of the annotations is altered, and the file saved. Following this, two of the text annotations are deleted, and the file saved again. Finally, three text annotations are added, and the file saved again.

The segments added to the file at each stage are shown separately. Throughout this example, objects are referred to by their object IDs, made up of the object number and generation number, rather than simply by the object number, as was done in earlier examples. This is necessary because objects are re-used in this example, so that the object number is not a unique identifier.

Note   *The tables in this section show only the objects that are modified at some point during the updating process. Objects from the example file in Section A.1, "Minimal PDF file" that are never altered during the update are not shown.*

A.6.1 Add four text annotations

Four text annotations were added to the initial file and the file saved.
Table A.4 lists the objects in this update.

Table A.4 *Object use after adding four text annotations*

Object ID	Object type
4 0	Page
7 0	Annots array
8 0	Text annotation
9 0	Text annotation
10 0	Text annotation
11 0	Text annotation

Example A.7 shows the lines added to the file by this update. The Page
object is updated because an **Annots** key has been added. Note that the
file's trailer now contains a **Prev** key, which points to the original cross-
reference section in the file, while the **startxref** value at the end of the
file points to the cross-reference section added by the update.

Example A.7 *Update section of PDF file when four text annotations are added*

```
4 0 obj
<<
/Type /Page
/Parent 3 0 R
/Resources << /ProcSet 6 0 R >>
/MediaBox [ 0 0 612 792 ]
/Contents 5 0 R
/Annots 7 0 R
>>
endobj
7 0 obj
[ 8 0 R 9 0 R 10 0 R 11 0 R ]
endobj
8 0 obj
<<
/Type /Annot
/Subtype /Text
/Open true
/Rect [ 44 616 162 735 ]
/Contents (Text #1)
>>
endobj
```

```
9 0 obj
<<
/Type /Annot
/Subtype /Text
/Open false
/Rect [ 224 668 457 735 ]
/Contents (Text #2)
>>
endobj
10 0 obj
<<
/Type /Annot
/Subtype /Text
/Open true
/Rect [ 239 393 328 622 ]
/Contents (Text #3)
>>
endobj
11 0 obj
<<
/Type /Annot
/Subtype /Text
/Open false
/Rect [ 34 398 225 575 ]
/Contents (Text #4)
>>
endobj
xref
0 1
0000000000 65535 f
4 1
0000000612 00000 n
7 5
0000000747 00000 n
0000000792 00000 n
0000000897 00000 n
0000001004 00000 n
0000001111 00000 n
trailer
<<
/Size 12
/Root 1 0 R
/Prev 408
>>
startxref
1218
%%EOF
```

A.6.2   Modify text of one annotation

The lines shown in Example A.8 were added to the file when it was saved after modifying one text annotation. Note that the file now contains two copies of the object with ID 10 0 (the text annotation that was modified), and that the cross-reference section added points to the more recent version of the object. The cross-reference section added contains one subsection. The subsection contains an entry only for the object that was modified. In addition, the **Prev** key in the file's trailer has been updated to point to the cross-reference section added by the previous update, while the **startxref** value at the end of the file points to the newly added cross-reference section.

Example A.8 *Update section of PDF file when one text annotation is modified*

```
10 0 obj
<<
/Type /Annot
/Subtype /Text
/Open true
/Rect [ 239 393 328 622 ]
/Contents (Modified Text #3)
>>
endobj
xref
10 1
0000001444 00000 n
trailer
<<
/Size 12
/Root 1 0 R
/Prev 1218
>>
startxref
1560
%%EOF
```

A.6.3   Delete two annotations

Table A.5 lists the objects updated when two text annotations were deleted and the file saved.

Table A.5 *Object use after deleting two text annotations*

Object ID	Object type
7 0	Annots array
8 0	Free
9 0	Free

The Annots array is the only object that is written in this update. It is updated because it now contains two fewer annotations.

Example A.9 shows the lines added when the file was saved. Note that objects with IDs 8 0 and 9 0 have been deleted, as can be seen from the fact that their entries in the cross-reference section end with an **f**. The cross-reference section added in this step contains four entries, corresponding to object number 0, the Annots array, and the two deleted text annotations. The cross-reference entry for object number 0 is updated because it is the head of the linked list of free objects, and must now point to the newly-freed entry for object number 8. The entry for object number 8 points to the entry for object number 9 (the next free entry), while the entry for object number 9 is the last free entry in the cross-reference table, indicated by the fact that it points to object number 0. The entries for the two deleted text annotations are marked as free, and as having generation numbers of 1, which will be used for any objects that re-use these cross-reference entries. Keep in mind that, although the two objects have been deleted, they are still present in the file. It is the cross-reference table that records the fact that they have been deleted.

The **Prev** key in the trailer dictionary has again been updated, so that it points to the cross-reference section added in the previous step, and the **startxref** value points to the newly added cross-reference section.

Example A.9 *Update section of PDF file when two text annotations are deleted*

```
7 0 obj
[ 10 0 R 11 0 R ]
endobj
xref
0 1
0000000008 65535 f
7 3
0000001658 00000 n
0000000009 00001 f
0000000000 00001 f
trailer
<<
/Size 12
/Root 1 0 R
/Prev 1560
>>
startxref
1691
%%EOF
```

A.6.4   Add three annotations

Finally, three text annotations were added to the file. Table A.6 lists the objects involved in this update.

Table A.6 *Object use after adding three text annotations*

Object ID	Object type
7 0	Annots array
8 1	Text annotation
9 1	Text annotation
12 0	Text annotation

Object numbers 8 and 9, which were the object numbers used for the two annotations deleted in the previous step, have been re-used. The new objects have been given a generation number of 1, however. In addition, the third text annotation added was assigned the previously unused object ID of 12 0.

Example A.10 shows the lines added to the file by this update. The cross-reference section added in this step contains five entries, corresponding object number 0, the Annots array, and the three annotations added. The entry for object number zero is updated because the previously free entries for object numbers 8 and 9 have been re-used. The entry for object number zero now shows that there are no free entries in the cross-reference table. The Annots array is updated to reflect the addition of the three new text annotations.

As in previous updates, the trailer's Prev key and **startxref** value have been updated.

The annotation with object ID 12 0 illustrates the splitting of a long text string across multiple lines, as well as the technique for including non-standard characters in a string. In this case, the character is an ellipsis (...), which is character code 203 (octal) in the **PDFDocEncoding** used for text annotations.

Example A.10 *Update section of PDF file after three text annotations are added*

```
7 0 obj
[ 10 0 R 11 0 R 8 1 R 9 1 R 12 0 R ]
endobj
8 1 obj
<<
/Type /Annot
/Subtype /Text
/Open true
/Rect [ 58 657 172 742 ]
/Contents (New Text #1)
>>
endobj
9 1 obj
<<
/Type /Annot
/Subtype /Text
/Open false
/Rect [ 389 459 570 537 ]
/Contents (New Text Annotation #2)
>>
endobj
12 0 obj
<<
/Type /Annot
/Subtype /Text
/Open true
/Rect [ 44 253 473 337 ]
/Contents (A longer annotation which we'll call, for lack of a better name\203New T\
ext #3)
>>
endobj
xref
```

```
0 1
0000000000 65535 f
7 3
0000001853 00000 n
0000001905 00001 n
0000002014 00001 n
12 1
0000002136 00000 n
trailer
<<
/Size 13
/Root 1 0 R
/Prev 1691
>>
startxref
2315
%%EOF
```

Summary of Page Marking Operators

Following is a list of all page marking operators used in PDF files, arranged alphabetically. For each operator, a brief description is given, along with a reference to the page in this document where the operator is discussed in detail. Words shown in boldface in the summary column are PostScript language operators.

Operator	Summary	Page
b	**closepath**, **fill** and **stroke** path	100
B	**fill** and **stroke** path	100
b*	**closepath**, **eofill**, and **stroke** path	100
B*	**eofill** and **stroke** path	100
BI	begin image	111
BT	begin text object	106
c	**curveto**	97
cm	**concat**. Concatenates the matrix to the current transformation matrix	94
d	**setdash**	94
d0	**setcharwidth** for Type 3 font	112
d1	**setcachedevice** for Type 3 font	112
Do	execute the named XObject	109
EI	end image	111
ET	end text object	106
f	**fill** path	100
f*	**eofill** path	100
g	**setgray** (fill)	95
G	**setgray** (stroke)	95
h	**closepath**	98
i	**setflat**	94
ID	begin image data	111
j	**setlinejoin**	94
J	**setlinecap**	94
k	**setcmykcolor** (fill)	95
K	**setcmykcolor** (stroke)	95
l	**lineto**	97
m	**moveto**	97
M	**setmiterlimit**	94
n	end path without **fill** or **stroke**	100
q	save graphics state	93
Q	restore graphics state	94
re	**rectangle**	98
rg	**setrgbcolor** (fill)	95
RG	**setrgbcolor** (stroke)	95
s	**closepath** and **stroke** path	100
S	**stroke** path	100
Tc	set character spacing	106
Td	move text current point	107
TD	move text current point and set leading	108

Operator	Summary	Page
Tf	set font name and size	107
Tj	show text	108
TJ	show text, allowing individual character positioning	109
TL	set leading	107
Tm	set text matrix	108
Tr	set text rendering mode	107
Ts	set super/subscripting text rise	107
Tw	set word spacing	107
Tz	set horizontal scaling	107
T*	move to start of next line	108
v	**curveto**	97
w	**setlinewidth**	94
W	**clip**	101
W*	**eoclip**	101
y	**curveto**	98
'	move to next line and show text	108
"	move to next line and show text	108

Predefined Font Encodings

PDF provides several predefined font encodings:

- **MacRomanEncoding**, **MacExpertEncoding**, and **WinAnsiEncoding** may be used in Font and Encoding objects.

- **PDFDocEncoding** is the encoding used in outline entries, text annotations, and strings in the Info dictionary.

- **StandardEncoding** is the built-in encoding for many fonts.

This appendix contains three tables describing these encodings. The first table shows all encodings except **MacExpertEncoding** and is arranged alphabetically by character name. The second table is similar, except that it is arranged numerically by character code. The third table shows the encoding for **MacExpertEncoding**, which is shown in a separate table because it has a substantially different character set than the other encodings.

C.1 Predefined encodings sorted by character name

Char	Name	StandardEncoding		MacRomanEncoding		WinAnsiEncoding		PDFDocEncoding	
		Decimal	Octal	Decimal	Octal	Decimal	Octal	Decimal	Octal
A	A	65	101	65	101	65	101	65	101
Æ	AE	225	341	174	256	198	306	198	306
Á	Aacute	—	—	231	347	193	301	193	301
Â	Acircumflex	—	—	229	345	194	302	194	302
Ä	Adieresis	—	—	128	200	196	304	196	304
À	Agrave	—	—	203	313	192	300	192	300
Å	Aring	—	—	129	201	197	305	197	305
Ã	Atilde	—	—	204	314	195	303	195	303
B	B	66	102	66	102	66	102	66	102
C	C	67	103	67	103	67	103	67	103
Ç	Ccedilla	—	—	130	202	199	307	199	307
D	D	68	104	68	104	68	104	68	104
E	E	69	105	69	105	69	105	69	105
É	Eacute	—	—	131	203	201	311	201	311
Ê	Ecircumflex	—	—	230	346	202	312	202	312
Ë	Edieresis	—	—	232	350	203	313	203	313
È	Egrave	—	—	233	351	200	310	200	310
Ð	Eth	—	—	—	—	208	320	208	320
F	F	70	106	70	106	70	106	70	106
G	G	71	107	71	107	71	107	71	107
H	H	72	110	72	110	72	110	72	110
I	I	73	111	73	111	73	111	73	111
Í	Iacute	—	—	234	352	205	315	205	315
Î	Icircumflex	—	—	235	353	206	316	206	316
Ï	Idieresis	—	—	236	354	207	317	207	317
Ì	Igrave	—	—	237	355	204	314	204	314
J	J	74	112	74	112	74	112	74	112
K	K	75	113	75	113	75	113	75	113
L	L	76	114	76	114	76	114	76	114
Ł	Lslash	232	350	—	—	—	—	149	225
M	M	77	115	77	115	77	115	77	115
N	N	78	116	78	116	78	116	78	116
Ñ	Ntilde	—	—	132	204	209	321	209	321
O	O	79	117	79	117	79	117	79	117
Œ	OE	234	352	206	316	140	214	150	226
Ó	Oacute	—	—	238	356	211	323	211	323
Ô	Ocircumflex	—	—	239	357	212	324	212	324

Char	Name	StandardEncoding		MacRomanEncoding		WinAnsiEncoding		PDFDocEncoding	
		Decimal	Octal	Decimal	Octal	Decimal	Octal	Decimal	Octal
Ö	Odieresis	—	—	133	205	214	326	214	326
Ò	Ograve	—	—	241	361	210	322	210	322
Ø	Oslash	233	351	175	257	216	330	216	330
Õ	Otilde	—	—	205	315	213	325	213	325
P	P	80	120	80	120	80	120	80	120
Q	Q	81	121	81	121	81	121	81	121
R	R	82	122	82	122	82	122	82	122
S	S	83	123	83	123	83	123	83	123
Š	Scaron	—	—	—	—	138	212	151	227
T	T	84	124	84	124	84	124	84	124
Þ	Thorn	—	—	—	—	222	336	222	336
U	U	85	125	85	125	85	125	85	125
Ú	Uacute	—	—	242	362	218	332	218	332
Û	Ucircumflex	—	—	243	363	219	333	219	333
Ü	Udieresis	—	—	134	206	220	334	220	334
Ù	Ugrave	—	—	244	364	217	331	217	331
V	V	86	126	86	126	86	126	86	126
W	W	87	127	87	127	87	127	87	127
X	X	88	130	88	130	88	130	88	130
Y	Y	89	131	89	131	89	131	89	131
Ý	Yacute	—	—	—	—	221	335	221	335
Ÿ	Ydieresis	—	—	217	331	159	237	152	230
Z	Z	90	132	90	132	90	132	90	132
Ž	Zcaron	—	—	—	—	—	—	153	231
a	a	97	141	97	141	97	141	97	141
á	aacute	—	—	135	207	225	341	225	341
â	acircumflex	—	—	137	211	226	342	226	342
´	acute	194	302	171	253	180	264	180	264
ä	adieresis	—	—	138	212	228	344	228	344
æ	ae	241	361	190	276	230	346	230	346
à	agrave	—	—	136	210	224	340	224	340
&	ampersand	38	46	38	46	38	46	38	46
å	aring	—	—	140	214	229	345	229	345
^	asciicircum	94	136	94	136	94	136	94	136
~	asciitilde	126	176	126	176	126	176	126	176
*	asterisk	42	52	42	52	42	52	42	52
@	at	64	100	64	100	64	100	64	100
ã	atilde	—	—	139	213	227	343	227	343
b	b	98	142	98	142	98	142	98	142

Char	Name	StandardEncoding		MacRomanEncoding		WinAnsiEncoding		PDFDocEncoding	
		Decimal	Octal	Decimal	Octal	Decimal	Octal	Decimal	Octal
\	backslash	92	134	92	134	92	134	92	134
|	bar	124	174	124	174	124	174	124	174
{	braceleft	123	173	123	173	123	173	123	173
}	braceright	125	175	125	175	125	175	125	175
[	bracketleft	91	133	91	133	91	133	91	133
]	bracketright	93	135	93	135	93	135	93	135
˘	breve	198	306	249	371	—	—	24	30
¦	brokenbar	—	—	—	—	166	246	166	246
•	bullet	183	267	165	245	149	225	128	200
c	c	99	143	99	143	99	143	99	143
ˇ	caron	207	317	255	377	—	—	25	31
ç	ccedilla	—	—	141	215	231	347	231	347
ˎ	cedilla	203	313	252	374	184	270	184	270
¢	cent	162	242	162	242	162	242	162	242
^	circumflex	195	303	246	366	136	210	26	32
:	colon	58	72	58	72	58	72	58	72
,	comma	44	54	44	54	44	54	44	54
©	copyright	—	—	169	251	169	251	169	251
¤	currency	168	250	219	333	164	244	164	244
d	d	100	144	100	144	100	144	100	144
†	dagger	178	262	160	240	134	206	129	201
‡	daggerdbl	179	263	224	340	135	207	130	202
°	degree	—	—	161	241	176	260	176	260
¨	dieresis	200	310	172	254	168	250	168	250
÷	divide	—	—	214	326	247	367	247	367
$	dollar	36	44	36	44	36	44	36	44
˙	dotaccent	199	307	250	372	—	—	27	33
ı	dotlessi	245	365	245	365	—	—	154	232
e	e	101	145	101	145	101	145	101	145
é	eacute	—	—	142	216	233	351	233	351
ê	ecircumflex	—	—	144	220	234	352	234	352
ë	edieresis	—	—	145	221	235	353	235	353
è	egrave	—	—	143	217	232	350	232	350
8	eight	56	70	56	70	56	70	56	70
…	ellipsis	188	274	201	311	133	205	131	203
—	emdash	208	320	209	321	151	227	132	204
–	endash	177	261	208	320	150	226	133	205
=	equal	61	75	61	75	61	75	61	75
ð	eth	—	—	—	—	240	360	240	360

Char	Name	StandardEncoding		MacRomanEncoding		WinAnsiEncoding		PDFDocEncoding	
		Decimal	Octal	Decimal	Octal	Decimal	Octal	Decimal	Octal
!	exclam	33	41	33	41	33	41	33	41
¡	exclamdown	161	241	193	301	161	241	161	241
f	f	102	146	102	146	102	146	102	146
fi	fi	174	256	222	336	—	—	147	223
5	five	53	65	53	65	53	65	53	65
fl	fl	175	257	223	337	—	—	148	224
f	florin	166	246	196	304	131	203	134	206
4	four	52	64	52	64	52	64	52	64
/	fraction	164	244	218	332	—	—	135	207
g	g	103	147	103	147	103	147	103	147
ß	germandbls	251	373	167	247	223	337	223	337
`	grave	193	301	96	140	96	140	96	140
>	greater	62	76	62	76	62	76	62	76
«	guillemotleft	171	253	199	307	171	253	171	253
»	guillemotright	187	273	200	310	187	273	187	273
‹	guilsinglleft	172	254	220	334	139	213	136	210
›	guilsinglright	173	255	221	335	155	233	137	211
h	h	104	150	104	150	104	150	104	150
˝	hungarumlaut	205	315	253	375	—	—	28	34
-	hyphen	45	55	45	55	45	55	45	55
i	i	105	151	105	151	105	151	105	151
í	iacute	—	—	146	222	237	355	237	355
î	icircumflex	—	—	148	224	238	356	238	356
ï	idieresis	—	—	149	225	239	357	239	357
ì	igrave	—	—	147	223	236	354	236	354
j	j	106	152	106	152	106	152	106	152
k	k	107	153	107	153	107	153	107	153
l	l	108	154	108	154	108	154	108	154
<	less	60	74	60	74	60	74	60	74
¬	logicalnot	—	—	194	302	172	254	172	254
ł	lslash	248	370	—	—	—	—	155	233
m	m	109	155	109	155	109	155	109	155
¯	macron	197	305	248	370	175	257	175	257
−	minus	—	—	—	—	—	—	138	212
μ	mu	—	—	181	265	181	265	181	265
×	multiply	—	—	—	—	215	327	215	327
n	n	110	156	110	156	110	156	110	156
9	nine	57	71	57	71	57	71	57	71
ñ	ntilde	—	—	150	226	241	361	241	361

Char	Name	StandardEncoding		MacRomanEncoding		WinAnsiEncoding		PDFDocEncoding	
		Decimal	Octal	Decimal	Octal	Decimal	Octal	Decimal	Octal
#	numbersign	35	43	35	43	35	43	35	43
o	o	111	157	111	157	111	157	111	157
ó	oacute	—	—	151	227	243	363	243	363
ô	ocircumflex	—	—	153	231	244	364	244	364
ö	odieresis	—	—	154	232	246	366	246	366
œ	oe	250	372	207	317	156	234	156	234
˛	ogonek	206	316	254	376	—	—	29	35
ò	ograve	—	—	152	230	242	362	242	362
1	one	49	61	49	61	49	61	49	61
½	onehalf	—	—	—	—	189	275	189	275
¼	onequarter	—	—	—	—	188	274	188	274
¹	onesuperior	—	—	—	—	185	271	185	271
ª	ordfeminine	227	343	187	273	170	252	170	252
º	ordmasculine	235	353	188	274	186	272	186	272
ø	oslash	249	371	191	277	248	370	248	370
õ	otilde	—	—	155	233	245	365	245	365
p	p	112	160	112	160	112	160	112	160
¶	paragraph	182	266	166	246	182	266	182	266
(	parenleft	40	50	40	50	40	50	40	50
)	parenright	41	51	41	51	41	51	41	51
%	percent	37	45	37	45	37	45	37	45
.	period	46	56	46	56	46	56	46	56
·	periodcentered	180	264	225	341	183	267	183	267
‰	perthousand	189	275	228	344	137	211	139	213
+	plus	43	53	43	53	43	53	43	53
±	plusminus	—	—	177	261	177	261	177	261
q	q	113	161	113	161	113	161	113	161
?	question	63	77	63	77	63	77	63	77
¿	questiondown	191	277	192	300	191	277	191	277
"	quotedbl	34	42	34	42	34	42	34	42
„	quotedblbase	185	271	227	343	132	204	140	214
"	quotedblleft	170	252	210	322	147	223	141	215
"	quotedblright	186	272	211	323	148	224	142	216
'	quoteleft	96	140	212	324	145	221	143	217
'	quoteright	39	47	213	325	146	222	144	220
‚	quotesinglbase	184	270	226	342	130	202	145	221
'	quotesingle	169	251	39	47	39	47	39	47
r	r	114	162	114	162	114	162	114	162
®	registered	—	—	168	250	174	256	174	256

Char	Name	StandardEncoding		MacRomanEncoding		WinAnsiEncoding		PDFDocEncoding	
		Decimal	Octal	Decimal	Octal	Decimal	Octal	Decimal	Octal
°	ring	202	312	251	373	176	260	30	36
s	s	115	163	115	163	115	163	115	163
š	scaron	—	—	—	—	154	232	157	235
§	section	167	247	164	244	167	247	167	247
;	semicolon	59	73	59	73	59	73	59	73
7	seven	55	67	55	67	55	67	55	67
6	six	54	66	54	66	54	66	54	66
/	slash	47	57	47	57	47	57	47	57
	space	32	40	32, 202	40,312	32	40	32	40
£	sterling	163	243	163	243	163	243	163	243
t	t	116	164	116	164	116	164	116	164
þ	thorn	—	—	—	—	254	376	254	376
3	three	51	63	51	63	51	63	51	63
¾	threequarters	—	—	—	—	190	276	190	276
³	threesuperior	—	—	—	—	179	263	179	263
~	tilde	196	304	247	367	152	230	31	37
™	trademark	—	—	170	252	153	231	146	222
2	two	50	62	50	62	50	62	50	62
²	twosuperior	—	—	—	—	178	262	178	262
u	u	117	165	117	165	117	165	117	165
ú	uacute	—	—	156	234	250	372	250	372
û	ucircumflex	—	—	158	236	251	373	251	373
ü	udieresis	—	—	159	237	252	374	252	374
ù	ugrave	—	—	157	235	249	371	249	371
_	underscore	95	137	95	137	95	137	95	137
v	v	118	166	118	166	118	166	118	166
w	w	119	167	119	167	119	167	119	167
x	x	120	170	120	170	120	170	120	170
y	y	121	171	121	171	121	171	121	171
ý	yacute	—	—	—	—	253	375	253	375
ÿ	ydieresis	—	—	216	330	255	377	255	377
¥	yen	165	245	180	264	165	245	165	245
z	z	122	172	122	172	122	172	122	172
ž	zcaron	—	—	—	—	—	—	158	236
0	zero	48	60	48	60	48	60	48	60

Note   *In the **WinAnsiEncoding**, the hyphen character can also be accessed using a character code of 173, the space using 160, and bullets are used for the otherwise unused character codes 127, 128, 129, 141, 142, 143, 144, 157, and 158.*

Note   Character codes 0 through 23 are not used in any of the predefined encodings.

Code		StandardEncoding	MacRomanEncoding	WinAnsiEncoding	PDFDocEncoding
Decimal	Octal				
24	30	—	—	—	breve
25	31	—	—	—	caron
26	32	—	—	—	circumflex
27	33	—	—	—	dotaccent
28	34	—	—	—	hungarumlaut
29	35	—	—	—	ogonek
30	36	—	—	—	ring
31	37	—	—	—	tilde
32	40	space	space	space	space
33	41	exclam	exclam	exclam	exclam
34	42	quotedbl	quotedbl	quotedbl	quotedbl
35	43	numbersign	numbersign	numbersign	numbersign
36	44	dollar	dollar	dollar	dollar
37	45	percent	percent	percent	percent
38	46	ampersand	ampersand	ampersand	ampersand
39	47	quoteright	quotesingle	quotesingle	quotesingle
40	50	parenleft	parenleft	parenleft	parenleft
41	51	parenright	parenright	parenright	parenright
42	52	asterisk	asterisk	asterisk	asterisk
43	53	plus	plus	plus	plus
44	54	comma	comma	comma	comma
45	55	hyphen	hyphen	hyphen	hyphen
46	56	period	period	period	period
47	57	slash	slash	slash	slash
48	60	zero	zero	zero	zero
49	61	one	one	one	one
50	62	two	two	two	two
51	63	three	three	three	three
52	64	four	four	four	four
53	65	five	five	five	five
54	66	six	six	six	six
55	67	seven	seven	seven	seven
56	70	eight	eight	eight	eight
57	71	nine	nine	nine	nine
58	72	colon	colon	colon	colon
59	73	semicolon	semicolon	semicolon	semicolon
60	74	less	less	less	less
61	75	equal	equal	equal	equal

Code		StandardEncoding	MacRomanEncoding	WinAnsiEncoding	PDFDocEncoding
Decimal	Octal				
62	76	greater	greater	greater	greater
63	77	question	question	question	question
64	100	at	at	at	at
65	101	A	A	A	A
66	102	B	B	B	B
67	103	C	C	C	C
68	104	D	D	D	D
69	105	E	E	E	E
70	106	F	F	F	F
71	107	G	G	G	G
72	110	H	H	H	H
73	111	I	I	I	I
74	112	J	J	J	J
75	113	K	K	K	K
76	114	L	L	L	L
77	115	M	M	M	M
78	116	N	N	N	N
79	117	O	O	O	O
80	120	P	P	P	P
81	121	Q	Q	Q	Q
82	122	R	R	R	R
83	123	S	S	S	S
84	124	T	T	T	T
85	125	U	U	U	U
86	126	V	V	V	V
87	127	W	W	W	W
88	130	X	X	X	X
89	131	Y	Y	Y	Y
90	132	Z	Z	Z	Z
91	133	bracketleft	bracketleft	bracketleft	bracketleft
92	134	backslash	backslash	backslash	backslash
93	135	bracketright	bracketright	bracketright	bracketright
94	136	asciicircum	asciicircum	asciicircum	asciicircum
95	137	underscore	underscore	underscore	underscore
96	140	quoteleft	grave	grave	grave
97	141	a	a	a	a
98	142	b	b	b	b
99	143	c	c	c	c
100	144	d	d	d	d
101	145	e	e	e	e
102	146	f	f	f	f
103	147	g	g	g	g

Code		StandardEncoding	MacRomanEncoding	WinAnsiEncoding	PDFDocEncoding
Decimal	Octal				
104	150	h	h	h	h
105	151	i	i	i	i
106	152	j	j	j	j
107	153	k	k	k	k
108	154	l	l	l	l
109	155	m	m	m	m
110	156	n	n	n	n
111	157	o	o	o	o
112	160	p	p	p	p
113	161	q	q	q	q
114	162	r	r	r	r
115	163	s	s	s	s
116	164	t	t	t	t
117	165	u	u	u	u
118	166	v	v	v	v
119	167	w	w	w	w
120	170	x	x	x	x
121	171	y	y	y	y
122	172	z	z	z	z
123	173	braceleft	braceleft	braceleft	braceleft
124	174	bar	bar	bar	bar
125	175	braceright	braceright	braceright	braceright
126	176	asciitilde	asciitilde	asciitilde	asciitilde
127	177	—	—	bullet	—
128	200	—	Adieresis	bullet	bullet
129	201	—	Aring	bullet	dagger
130	202	—	Ccedilla	quotesinglbase	daggerdbl
131	203	—	Eacute	florin	ellipsis
132	204	—	Ntilde	quotedblbase	emdash
133	205	—	Odieresis	ellipsis	endash
134	206	—	Udieresis	dagger	florin
135	207	—	aacute	daggerdbl	fraction
136	210	—	agrave	circumflex	guilsinglleft
137	211	—	acircumflex	perthousand	guilsinglright
138	212	—	adieresis	Scaron	minus
139	213	—	atilde	guilsinglleft	perthousand
140	214	—	aring	OE	quotedblbase
141	215	—	ccedilla	bullet	quotedblleft
142	216	—	eacute	bullet	quotedblright
143	217	—	egrave	bullet	quoteleft
144	220	—	ecircumflex	bullet	quoteright
145	221	—	edieresis	quoteleft	quotesinglbase

Code		StandardEncoding	MacRomanEncoding	WinAnsiEncoding	PDFDocEncoding
Decimal	Octal				
146	222	—	iacute	quoteright	trademark
147	223	—	igrave	quotedblleft	fi
148	224	—	icircumflex	quotedblright	fl
149	225	—	idieresis	bullet	Lslash
150	226	—	ntilde	endash	OE
151	227	—	oacute	emdash	Scaron
152	230	—	ograve	tilde	Ydieresis
153	231	—	ocircumflex	trademark	Zcaron
154	232	—	odieresis	scaron	dotlessi
155	233	—	otilde	guilsinglright	lslash
156	234	—	uacute	oe	oe
157	235	—	ugrave	bullet	scaron
158	236	—	ucircumflex	bullet	zcaron
159	237	—	udieresis	Ydieresis	—
160	240	—	dagger	space	—
161	241	exclamdown	degree	exclamdown	exclamdown
162	242	cent	cent	cent	cent
163	243	sterling	sterling	sterling	sterling
164	244	fraction	section	currency	currency
165	245	yen	bullet	yen	yen
166	246	florin	paragraph	brokenbar	brokenbar
167	247	section	germandbls	section	section
168	250	currency	registered	dieresis	dieresis
169	251	quotesingle	copyright	copyright	copyright
170	252	quotedblleft	trademark	ordfeminine	ordfeminine
171	253	guillemotleft	acute	guillemotleft	guillemotleft
172	254	guilsinglleft	dieresis	logicalnot	logicalnot
173	255	guilsinglright	—	hyphen	—
174	256	fi	AE	registered	registered
175	257	fl	Oslash	macron	macron
176	260	—	—	degree	degree
177	261	endash	plusminus	plusminus	plusminus
178	262	dagger	—	twosuperior	twosuperior
179	263	daggerdbl	—	threesuperior	threesuperior
180	264	periodcentered	yen	acute	acute
181	265	—	mu	mu	mu
182	266	paragraph	—	paragraph	paragraph
183	267	bullet	—	periodcentered	periodcentered
184	270	quotesinglbase	—	cedilla	cedilla
185	271	quotedblbase	—	onesuperior	onesuperior
186	272	quotedblright	—	ordmasculine	ordmasculine
187	273	guillemotright	ordfeminine	guillemotright	guillemotright

Code		StandardEncoding	MacRomanEncoding	WinAnsiEncoding	PDFDocEncoding
Decimal	Octal				
188	274	ellipsis	ordmasculine	onequarter	onequarter
189	275	perthousand	—	onehalf	onehalf
190	276	—	ae	threequarters	threequarters
191	277	questiondown	oslash	questiondown	questiondown
192	300	—	questiondown	Agrave	Agrave
193	301	grave	exclamdown	Aacute	Aacute
194	302	acute	logicalnot	Acircumflex	Acircumflex
195	303	circumflex	—	Atilde	Atilde
196	304	tilde	florin	Adieresis	Adieresis
197	305	macron	—	Aring	Aring
198	306	breve	—	AE	AE
199	307	dotaccent	guillemotleft	Ccedilla	Ccedilla
200	310	dieresis	guillemotright	Egrave	Egrave
201	311	—	ellipsis	Eacute	Eacute
202	312	ring	space	Ecircumflex	Ecircumflex
203	313	cedilla	Agrave	Edieresis	Edieresis
204	314	—	Atilde	Igrave	Igrave
205	315	hungarumlaut	Otilde	Iacute	Iacute
206	316	ogonek	OE	Icircumflex	Icircumflex
207	317	caron	oe	Idieresis	Idieresis
208	320	emdash	endash	Eth	Eth
209	321	—	emdash	Ntilde	Ntilde
210	322	—	quotedblleft	Ograve	Ograve
211	323	—	quotedblright	Oacute	Oacute
212	324	—	quoteleft	Ocircumflex	Ocircumflex
213	325	—	quoteright	Otilde	Otilde
214	326	—	divide	Odieresis	Odieresis
215	327	—	—	multiply	multiply
216	330	—	ydieresis	Oslash	Oslash
217	331	—	Ydieresis	Ugrave	Ugrave
218	332	—	fraction	Uacute	Uacute
219	333	—	currency	Ucircumflex	Ucircumflex
220	334	—	guilsinglleft	Udieresis	Udieresis
221	335	—	guilsinglright	Yacute	Yacute
222	336	—	fi	Thorn	Thorn
223	337	—	fl	germandbls	germandbls
224	340	—	daggerdbl	agrave	agrave
225	341	AE	periodcentered	aacute	aacute
226	342	—	quotesinglbase	acircumflex	acircumflex
227	343	ordfeminine	quotedblbase	atilde	atilde
228	344	—	perthousand	adieresis	adieresis
229	345	—	Acircumflex	aring	aring

Code		StandardEncoding	MacRomanEncoding	WinAnsiEncoding	PDFDocEncoding
Decimal	Octal				
230	346	—	Ecircumflex	ae	ae
231	347	—	Aacute	ccedilla	ccedilla
232	350	Lslash	Edieresis	egrave	egrave
233	351	Oslash	Egrave	eacute	eacute
234	352	OE	Iacute	ecircumflex	ecircumflex
235	353	ordmasculine	Icircumflex	edieresis	edieresis
236	354	—	Idieresis	igrave	igrave
237	355	—	Igrave	iacute	iacute
238	356	—	Oacute	icircumflex	icircumflex
239	357	—	Ocircumflex	idieresis	idieresis
240	360	—	—	eth	eth
241	361	ae	Ograve	ntilde	ntilde
242	362	—	Uacute	ograve	ograve
243	363	—	Ucircumflex	oacute	oacute
244	364	—	Ugrave	ocircumflex	ocircumflex
245	365	dotlessi	dotlessi	otilde	otilde
246	366	—	circumflex	odieresis	odieresis
247	367	—	tilde	divide	divide
248	370	lslash	macron	oslash	oslash
249	371	oslash	breve	ugrave	ugrave
250	372	oe	dotaccent	uacute	uacute
251	373	germandbls	ring	ucircumflex	ucircumflex
252	374	—	cedilla	udieresis	udieresis
253	375	—	hungarumlaut	yacute	yacute
254	376	—	ogonek	thorn	thorn
255	377	—	caron	ydieresis	ydieresis

C.3 MacExpert encoding

Char	Name	Code Decimal	Code Octal	Char	Name	Code Decimal	Code Octal
Æ	AEsmall	190	276	Ł	Lslashsmall	194	302
Á	Aacutesmall	135	207	L	Lsmall	108	154
Â	Acircumflexsmall	137	211	¯	Macronsmall	244	364
´	Acutesmall	39	47	M	Msmall	109	155
Ä	Adieresissmall	138	212	N	Nsmall	110	156
À	Agravesmall	136	210	Ñ	Ntildesmall	150	226
Å	Aringsmall	140	214	Œ	OEsmall	207	317
A	Asmall	97	141	Ó	Oacutesmall	151	227
Ã	Atildesmall	139	213	Ô	Ocircumflexsmall	153	231
˘	Brevesmall	243	363	Ö	Odieresissmall	154	232
B	Bsmall	98	142	˛	Ogoneksmall	242	362
ˇ	Caronsmall	174	256	Ò	Ogravesmall	152	230
Ç	Ccedillasmall	141	215	Ø	Oslashsmall	191	277
¸	Cedillasmall	201	311	O	Osmall	111	157
^	Circumflexsmall	94	136	Õ	Otildesmall	155	233
C	Csmall	99	143	P	Psmall	112	160
¨	Dieresissmall	172	254	Q	Qsmall	113	161
˙	Dotaccentsmall	250	372	°	Ringsmall	251	373
D	Dsmall	100	144	R	Rsmall	114	162
É	Eacutesmall	142	216	Š	Scaronsmall	167	247
Ê	Ecircumflexsmall	144	220	S	Ssmall	115	163
Ë	Edieresissmall	145	221	Þ	Thornsmall	185	271
È	Egravesmall	143	217	˜	Tildesmall	126	176
E	Esmall	101	145	T	Tsmall	116	164
Ð	Ethsmall	68	104	Ú	Uacutesmall	156	234
F	Fsmall	102	146	Û	Ucircumflexsmall	158	236
`	Gravesmall	96	140	Ü	Udieresissmall	159	237
G	Gsmall	103	147	Ù	Ugravesmall	157	235
H	Hsmall	104	150	U	Usmall	117	165
˝	Hungarumlautsmall	34	42	V	Vsmall	118	166
Í	Iacutesmall	146	222	W	Wsmall	119	167
Î	Icircumflexsmall	148	224	X	Xsmall	120	170
Ï	Idieresissmall	149	225	Ý	Yacutesmall	180	264
Ì	Igravesmall	147	223	Ÿ	Ydieresissmall	216	330
I	Ismall	105	151	Y	Ysmall	121	171
J	Jsmall	106	152	Ž	Zcaronsmall	189	275
K	Ksmall	107	153	Z	Zsmall	122	172

Char	Name	Code Decimal	Code Octal	Char	Name	Code Decimal	Code Octal
&	ampersandsmall	38	46	l	lsuperior	241	361
a	asuperior	129	201	m	msuperior	247	367
b	bsuperior	245	365	9	nineinferior	187	273
¢	centinferior	169	251	9	nineoldstyle	57	71
¢	centoldstyle	35	43	9	ninesuperior	225	341
¢	centsuperior	130	202	n	nsuperior	246	366
:	colon	58	72	.	onedotenleader	43	53
₵	colonmonetary	123	173	⅛	oneeighth	74	112
,	comma	44	54	1	onefitted	124	174
,	commainferior	178	262	½	onehalf	72	110
'	commasuperior	248	370	1	oneinferior	193	301
$	dollarinferior	182	266	I	oneoldstyle	49	61
$	dollaroldstyle	36	44	¼	onequarter	71	107
$	dollarsuperior	37	45	1	onesuperior	218	332
d	dsuperior	235	353	⅓	onethird	78	116
8	eightinferior	165	245	o	osuperior	175	257
8	eightoldstyle	56	70	(	parenleftinferior	91	133
8	eightsuperior	161	241	(	parenleftsuperior	40	50
e	esuperior	228	344	)	parenrightinferior	93	135
¡	exclamdownsmall	214	326	)	parenrightsuperior	41	51
!	exclamsmall	33	41	.	period	46	56
ff	ff	86	126	.	periodinferior	179	263
ffi	ffi	89	131	·	periodsuperior	249	371
ffl	ffl	90	132	¿	questiondownsmall	192	300
fi	fi	87	127	?	questionsmall	63	77
–	figuredash	208	320	r	rsuperior	229	345
⅝	fiveeighths	76	114	Rp	rupiah	125	175
5	fiveinferior	176	260	;	semicolon	59	73
5	fiveoldstyle	53	65	⅞	seveneighths	77	115
5	fivesuperior	222	336	7	seveninferior	166	246
fl	fl	88	130	7	sevenoldstyle	55	67
4	fourinferior	162	242	7	sevensuperior	224	340
4	fouroldstyle	52	64	6	sixinferior	164	244
4	foursuperior	221	335	6	sixoldstyle	54	66
/	fraction	47	57	6	sixsuperior	223	337
-	hyphen	45	55		space	32	40
-	hypheninferior	95	137	s	ssuperior	234	352
-	hyphensuperior	209	321	⅜	threeeighths	75	113
i	isuperior	233	351	3	threeinferior	163	243

Char	Name	Code		Char	Name	Code	
		Decimal	Octal			Decimal	Octal
3	threeoldstyle	51	63				
¾	threequarters	73	111				
—	threequartersemdash	61	75				
3	threesuperior	220	334				
t	tsuperior	230	346				
..	twodotenleader	42	52				
2	twoinferior	170	252				
2	twooldstyle	50	62				
2	twosuperior	219	333				
⅔	twothirds	79	117				
0	zeroinferior	188	274				
o	zerooldstyle	48	60				
0	zerosuperior	226	342				

APPENDIX D

Implementation Limits

In general, PDF does not restrict the size or quantity of things described in the file format, such as numbers, arrays, images, and so on. However, a PDF viewer application running on a particular processor and in a particular operating environment does have such limits. If a viewer application attempts to perform an action that exceeds one of the limits, it will display an error.

PostScript interpreters also have implementation limits, listed in Appendix B of the *PostScript Language Reference Manual, Second Edition*. It is possible to construct a PDF file that does not violate viewer application limits but will not print on a PostScript printer. Keep in mind that these limits vary according to the PostScript language level, interpreter version, and the amount of memory available to the interpreter.

All limits are sufficiently large that most PDF files should never approach them. However, using the techniques described in Chapters 8 through 12 of this book will further reduce the chance of reaching these limits.

This appendix describes typical limits for Acrobat Exchange and Acrobat Reader. These limits fall into two main classes:

- *Architectural limits.* The hardware on which a viewer application executes imposes certain constraints. For example, an integer is usually represented in 32 bits, limiting the range of allowed integers. In addition, the design of the software imposes other constraints, such as a limit of 65535 elements in an array or string.

- *Memory limits.* The amount of memory available to a viewer application limits the number of memory-consuming objects that can be held simultaneously.

PDF itself has one architectural limit. Because ten digits are allocated to byte offsets, the size of a file is limited to 10^{10} bytes (approximately 10GB.)

Table D.1 describes the architectural limits for most PDF viewer applications running on 32-bit machines. These limits are likely to remain constant across a wide variety of implementations. However, memory limits will often be exceeded before architectural limits, such as the limit on the number of PDF objects, are reached.

Table D.1 *Architectural limits*

Quantity	Limit	Explanation
integer	2147483647	Largest positive value, $2^{31} - 1$.
	−2147483648	Largest negative value, -2^{31}.
real	±32767	Approximate range of values.
	±1/65536	Approximate smallest non-zero value.
	5	Approximate number of decimal digits of precision in fractional part.
array	65535	Maximum number of elements in an array.
dictionary	65535	Maximum number of key–value pairs in a dictionary.
string	65535	Maximum number of characters in a string.
name	127	Maximum number of characters in a name.
indirect object	250000	Maximum number of indirect objects in a PDF file.

Memory limits cannot be characterized so precisely, because the amount of available memory and the way in which it is allocated vary from one implementation to another.

Memory is automatically reallocated from one use to another when necessary. When more memory is needed for a particular purpose, it can be taken away from memory allocated to another purpose if that memory is currently unused or its use is non-essential (a cache, for example.) Also, data is often saved to a temporary file when memory is limited. Because of this behavior, it is not possible to state limits for such items as the number of pages, number of text annotations or hypertext links on a page, number of graphics objects on a page, or number of fonts on a page or in a document.

Version 1.0 of Acrobat Exchange and Acrobat Reader have some additional architectural limits:

- Thumbnails may be no larger than 106×106 samples, and should be created at one-eighth scale for 8-1/2×11 inch and A4 size pages. Thumbnails should use either the **DeviceGray** or direct or indexed **DeviceRGB** color space.

- The minimum allowed page size is 1×1 inch (72×72 units in the default user space coordinate system), and the maximum allowed page size is 45×45 inches (3240×3240 units in the default user space coordinate system).

- The zoom factor of a view is constrained to be between .12 (12%) and 8 (800%), regardless of the zoom factor specified in the PDF file.

- When Acrobat Exchange or Acrobat Reader reads a PDF file with a damaged or missing cross-reference table, it attempts to rebuild the table by scanning all the objects in the file. However, the generation numbers of deleted entries are lost if the cross-reference table is missing or severely damaged. Reconstruction fails if any object identifiers do not occur at the start of a line or if the **endobj** keyword does not appear at the start of a line. Also, reconstruction fails if a stream contains a line beginning with the word **endstream**, aside from the required **endstream** that delimits the end of the stream.

Obtaining XUIDs and Technical Notes

Creators of widely distributed forms who wish to use the XUID mechanism must obtain an organization ID from Adobe Systems Incorporated at the addresses listed below.

Technical notes, technical support, and periodic mailings are available to members of the Adobe Developers Association. In particular, the PostScript language software development kit (SDK) contains all the technical notes mentioned in this book. The Adobe Developers Association can be contacted at the addresses listed below:

Europe:
Adobe Developers Association
Adobe Systems Europe B.V.
Europlaza
Hoogoorddreef 54a
1101 BE Amsterdam Z-O
The Netherlands
Telephone: +31 20 6511 200
Fax: +31 20 6511 300

U.S. and the rest of the world:
Adobe Developers Association
Adobe Systems Incorporated
1585 Charleston Road
P.O. Box 7900
Mountain View, CA 94039-7900
Telephone: (415) 961–4111
Fax: (415) 969–4138

In addition, some technical notes and other information may be available from an anonymous ftp site, ftp.adobe.com (130.248.1.4). When accessing the anonymous ftp site, use "anonymous" as the user name, and provide your E-mail address as the password (for example, smith@adobe.com). For users without access to ftp, the information available from the ftp site is also available via a mailserver which may be contacted at the addresses:

ps-file-server@adobe.com (internet)
{sun,decwrl,apple}!adobe!ps-file-server (uucp)

To obtain additional information on using the mailserver, send a message using the word "help" as the subject line and with nothing in the body of the message. The mailserver and the ftp site do not contain clip art, fonts, or end-user programs.

Bibliography

Adobe Systems Incorporated, *PostScript Language Reference Manual, Second Edition*, Addison-Wesley, 1990, ISBN 0-201-10174-2. Reference manual describing the imaging model used in the PostScript language and the language itself.

Adobe Systems Incorporated, *Supporting Data Compression in PostScript Level 2 and the Filter Operator*, Adobe Developer Support Technical Note 5115.

Adobe Systems Incorporated, *Supporting the DCT Filters in PostScript Level 2*, Adobe Developer Support Technical Note 5116. Contains errata for the JPEG discussion in the *PostScript Language Reference Manual, Second Edition*. Also describes the compatibility of the JPEG implementation with various versions of the JPEG standard.

Adobe Systems Incorporated, *Adobe Type 1 Font Format*, Addison-Wesley, 1990, ISBN 0-201-57044-0. Explains the internal organization of a PostScript language Type 1 font program.

Adobe Systems Incorporated, *Adobe Type 1 Font Format: Multiple Master Extensions*, Adobe Developer Support Technical Note 5086. Describes the additions made to the Type 1 font format to support multiple master fonts.

Aho, Alfred V., John E. Hopcroft, and Jeffrey D. Ullman, *Data Structures and Algorithms*, Addison-Wesley, 1983, ISBN 0-201-00023-7. Includes a discussion of balanced trees.

Arvo, James (ed.), *Graphics Gems II*, Academic Press, 1991, ISBN 0-12-064480-0. The section "Geometrically Continuous Cubic Bézier Curves" by Hans-Peter Seidel describes the mathematics used to smoothly join two cubic Bézier curves.

CCITT, *Blue Book*, Volume VII.3, 1988. ISBN 92-61-03611-2. Recommendations T.4 and T.6 are the CCITT standards for Group 3 and Group 4 facsimile encoding. This document may be purchased from Global Engineering Documents, P.O. Box 19539, Irvine, California 92713.

Foley, James D. , Andries van Dam, Steven K. Feiner, and John F. Hughes, *Computer Graphics: Principles and Practice, Second Edition,*. Addison-Wesley, 1990, ISBN 0-201-12110-7. Section 11.2, "Parametric Cubic Curves", contains a description of the mathematics of cubic Bézier curves and a comparison of various types of parametric cubic curves.

Glassner, Andrew S. (ed.), *Graphics Gems*, Academic Press, 1990, ISBN 0-12-286165-5. The section "An Algorithm For Automatically Fitting Digitized Curves" by Philip J. Schneider describes an algorithm for determining the set of Bézier curves approximating an arbitrary set of user-provided points. Appendix 2 contains an implementation of the algorithm, written in the C programming language. Other sections relevant to the mathematics of Bézier curves include "Solving the Nearest-Point-On-Curve Problem" by Philip J. Schneider, "Some Properties of Bézier Curves" by Ronald Goldman, and "A Bézier Curve-Based Root-Finder" by Philip J. Schneider. The source code appearing in the appendix is available via anonymous ftp, as described in the preface to *Graphics Gems III*.

Joint Photographic Experts Group (JPEG) "Revision 8 of the JPEG Technical Specification," ISO/IEC JTC1/SC2/WG8, CCITT SGVIII, August 14, 1990. Defines a set of still picture grayscale and color image data compression algorithms.

Kirk, David (ed.), *Graphics Gems III*, Academic Press, 1992, ISBN 0-12-409670-0 (with IBM Disk) or ISBN 0-12-409671-9 (with Macintosh disk). The section "Interpolation Using Bézier Curves" by Gershon Elber contains an algorithm for calculating a Bézier curve that passes through a user-specified set of points. The algorithm utilizes not only cubic Bézier curves, which are supported in PDF, but also higher-order Bézier curves. The appendix contains an implementation of the algorithm, written in the C programming language. All of the source code appearing in the appendix is available via anonymous ftp, as described in the preface.

Pennebaker, W. B. and Joan L. Mitchell, *JPEG Still Image Data Compression Standard*, Van Nostrand Reinhold, 1993, ISBN 0-442-01272-1.

Warnock, J. and D. Wyatt, "A Device Independent Graphics Imaging Model for Use with Raster Devices," *Computer Graphics* (ACM SIGGRAPH), Volume 16, Number 3, July 1982. Technical background for the imaging model used in the PostScript language.

Index

precision of real numbers, 117–118
Predictor key, for LZW filter, 34
Prev key
    for outline entry, 59
    for trailer, 46, 173, 175, 176
printer drivers, PDF Writer as, 6
ProcSet resources, 12, 61–62, 144, 159
    sharing, 119
Producer key, for info dictionary, 83

Q

Q operator, 94, 118, 127, 155
q operator, 93, 118, 127, 155

R

R keyword, for indirect object reference, 39
radial blends, 156
re operator, 98, 133
real numbers, 25
    limits, 202
    precision of, 117–118
Rect key
    for link annotations, 57
    for text annotations, 56
rectangle operator, 98, 135
red–green–blue (RGB) color space, 95
resolution, 137. *See also output device resolution*
resource dictionary, for page object, 54, 155
resources, 60–83
    color space, 76–77
    encoding, 69–70
    fonts, 62–69
    form, 81–83
    image, 55, 78–81
    names, 114
    ProcSet, 61–62
    sharing, 119
    XObject, 78
Resources key
    for form, 82
    for Page object, 53
RG operator, 95
rg operator, 95
right parenthesis, escape sequence, 26
Root key, for trailer, 46, 50
root node
    for document, 50
    for Pages tree, 51, 52
    for outline, 51, 58

Rotate key, for Page object, 53
rotations, 20, 137
round joins, 92
Rows key, for CCITTFaxDecode filter, 36
Run Length compression filter, 9
RunLengthDecode filter, 30, 35, 111, 143

S

S operator, 100, 146
s operator, 100, 155
scale factor for fonts, 18
scaling, 19, 20
screenshot, compression of, 140
script font, font flag for, 74
serif font, font flag for, 74
setcachedevice operator, 112
setcharwidth operator, 112
setcmykcolor operator, 95
setdash operator, 94
setflat operator, 94
setgray operator, 95
setlinecap operator, 94
setlinejoin operator, 94
setlinewidth operator, 94
setmiterlimit operator, 94
setrgbcolor operator, 95
sharing objects, 115
sharing resources, 119
Size key, for trailer, 46
skew, 20, 137
small cap fonts, font flag for, 74
spacing
    text, 125
    between words, 87, 105, 107, 109, 125, 127
stack, for graphics state, 88
StandardEncoding, 185–197
startxref keyword, 46, 173, 175, 176
StemH key, for font descriptor, 72
StemV key, for font descriptor, 71
stream keyword, 29
streams, 29–38
string objects, 26. *See also text string*
    spaces in, 126
    vs. streams, 29
stroke, 86, 98
    dash pattern in, 91
stroke color, 87, 93, 131
stroke operator, 100, 116
subpath, closing, 98, 99
subscripts, 105, 107

Subtype key
    for form, 82
    for image resources, 79
    for link annotations, 57
    for multiple master Type 1 font, 66
    for text annotations, 56
    for TrueType fonts, 68
    for Type 1 fonts, 64
    for Type 3 fonts, 67
superscripts, 105, 107
symbolic fonts, 10
    font flag for, 74

T

T* operator, 108, 122–123, 127
Tc operator, 106, 125
TD operator, 108, 122, 124, 127, 107, 127, 149, 155
text
    as clipping path, 147–149
    example PDF file, 161
    justified, 129
    LZW filter to compress, 33
    optimizing, 121–129
    spacing, 125
text annotations, 56
text font, 87, 103
text matrix, 87, 103
text objects, 86
    avoiding unnecessary, 121–122
text operators, 106–109
    for positioning, 107–108, 127
    selecting, 126–127
Text ProcSet, 62
text rendering mode, 87, 104, 107, 122, 155
text rise, 87, 105, 107
text size, 87, 105, 107
text space, 18
    transformation to user space, 103
text state, 101–105
text string
    limits, 202
    operators, 108–109
    splitting, 26, 178
Tf operator, 107, 149, 155
Thumb key, for page object, 53
thumbnail sketches, 55
    displaying, 50
    limitations, 203
Title key, for outline entry, 59
TJ operator, 109, 126

Colophon

This book was produced electronically using FrameMaker® on the Macintosh, NeXT™, and Sun™ SPARCstation™ computers. Art was produced using Adobe Photoshop™ and Adobe Illustrator on the Macintosh. Film was produced with the PostScript language on an Agfa-Compugraphic SelectSet™ 5000 imagesetter.

The type used is from the ITC Stone® family. Heads are set in ITC Stone Sans Semibold and the body text is set in 9 on 12 point ITC Stone Serif, ITC Stone Serif Italic, and ITC Stone Sans Semibold.

Authors—Tim Bienz, Richard Cohn

Key Contributors—Alan Wootton, Nabeel Al-Shamma

Editor—Diana Wynne

Illustrations and Book Production—Lauren Buchholz

Cover Design—Nancy Winters

Reviewers—Nabeel Al-Shamma, David Gelphman, Sherri Nichols, Paul Rovner, Alan Wootton, and numerous others at Adobe Systems.

Publication Management—Patrick Ames

Project Management—Rob Babcock, Bob Wulff